William Clark

Jeffersonian Man on the Frontier

William Clark, portrait by Joseph H. Bush *(Courtesy The Filson Club)*

William Clark

JEFFERSONIAN MAN ON THE FRONTIER

by Jerome O. Steffen

UNIVERSITY OF OKLAHOMA PRESS

NORMAN

Library of Congress Cataloging in Publication Data

Steffen, Jerome O   1942–
    William Clark: Jeffersonian man on the frontier.

    Bibliography: p.
    Includes index.
    1. Clark, William, 1770–1838. 2. Indians of North
America—Government relations—1789–1869.
F592.C56S74   917.8'04'20924 [B]   76–15355
    ISBN: 0–8061–1373–1

For Gloria

Preface

This is not an orthodox biography. It is, rather, a selective analysis of William Clark's life as that life reflects broader themes of early nineteenth-century America. Usually Clark's name is associated exclusively with the Lewis and Clark Expedition. From his birth in 1770 to his death in 1838, however, he lived a long, varied, and distinguished life. As businessman, politician, and federal Indian official, Clark lived through a period of significant economic, political, social, and intellectual change that directly affected the course of his life. His biography, then, provides a vehicle for analyzing that change from a national perspective as well as from the perspective of one individual's association with the broader forces affecting his life.

In examining Clark's life, I have weighed the relationship between historical forces and the dynamics of change. In a comparative sense, I have asked, how do individuals and mass society relate to change? For example, much that affected William Clark's life and others of his time was unknown to them. The realm of the conscious-versus-unconscious perception of reality becomes a major dimension in understanding individual as well as national history. In other words, is man the architect of his destiny or is he merely swept along with history? In *The Acceptance of*

Histories: Toward a Perspective for Social Sciences, Kenneth Bock suggests the latter when he states that the "Historical study of ideas serves a need that cannot be met by merely critical or logical analysis. The ideas to which we pay conscious homage are not necessarily those that most strongly guide our thinking."

Most historians would agree that history vacillates between periods when individuals, at least in the short-run, can effectively orchestrate their lives with some degree of confidence in tradition and periods when tradition is swept aside by pressing forces not in their control or even understood. These factors, when placed in the context of Clark's life, suggest that the America of his early years was a place where traditional ideas and practices in the conscious realm relinquished themselves slowly to the pressures of contrary external forces. On the other hand, the America of Clark's later years was a place where tradition was swept aside by external pressures and became subordinate to the dictates of the immediate and practical.

An introspective biography of William Clark, such as I have outlined, poses a problem. Traditionally, historians have written intellectual biographies only about intellectuals. This is understandable because the intellectual is most likely to articulate a world view through prose, poetry, and oratory. Hence it is a simple matter for the historian to gather, organize, and present these views in an orderly narrative fashion. Is it possible, however, to analyze, from an intellectual perspective, the life of an individual who does not articulate his world view? I contend that it is, if one keeps in mind that individual actions are not performed in isolation and that they are representative of ideas and values. Behavior, when viewed accumulatively, can present a compelling and patterned intellectual picture of human personality development. For example, Clark never wrote, "I am an Enlightenment man.

I have read Locke, Hume, and Diderot, and these are the
principles that comprise my world view." However, when
the patterned totality of his life is examined, it becomes
apparent through his actions that he is indeed saying, "My
life was deeply affected by Enlightenment ideas and Jeffersonian principles."

This book could not have been written without the help
of many individuals. I wish to express my deepest gratitude to Lewis Atherton, whose encouragement throughout
my career has been an inspiration. I am deeply indebted
to his wise counseling and many thoughtful suggestions.
I would also like to thank William W. Savage, Jr. and H.
Wayne Morgan whose critical and insightful comments
prevented me from making many errors of judgment. My
indebtedness also extends to James R. Bently, Curator of
Manuscripts at the Filson Club in Louisville, Kentucky; to
Mrs. Ernst Stadler, Archivist at the Missouri Historical
Society Jefferson Memorial in St. Louis; and to Mrs. Nancy
Prewitt, Assistant Director of the Western Historical
Manuscripts Collection in Columbia, Missouri, for their
invaluable assistance in locating pertinent manuscript
collections. In addition, I would like to thank the Woodrow
Wilson National Fellowship Foundation and the National
Endowment for the Humanities, whose funds have enabled me to complete this work. Special thanks are due
also to Mrs. Myrtle Berkley, Alexis Rodgers, and Cathye
Woody who typed the manuscript with a keen editorial
eye. Finally, there is my wife, Gloria Roth Steffen, without whose patience and encouragement this study could
not have been completed.

Parts of Chapters III and VII, in different versions,
have been published respectively in *Montana the Magazine of Western History*, Vol. XXV (Spring, 1975), 52–61,
and the *Missouri Historical Review*, Vol. LXVII (January,
1973), 171–197.

Contents

Illustrations

William Clark

Jeffersonian Man on the Frontier

I
Introduction

Villiam Clark was a product of eighteenth-century Virginia, the place where American Enlightenment blossomed most fully. Clark absorbed the values of that time and place, and they profoundly influenced his life as a Jeffersonian Republican.[1] But neither the total spectre of the American Enlightenment nor the encompassing nature of Jeffersonian Republicanism are responsible for the ethos of William Clark. There are, however, strong undercurrents in each that help to illuminate the three main activities of his life—western exploration, territorial politics, and the adminstration of Indian policy.

Although historians of the Enlightenment point to the diversity of the movement—some even doubt its existence in the New World—certain of its tenets are seldom questioned.[2] Most agree that the core of Enlightenment thought is the rejection of mysticism and an adherence to experience and reason as the basis for all knowledge. On one of the few occasions when Clark demonstrated his leanings in philosophical terms, he revealed the very essence of Enlightenment thinking. The frontispiece of one of his early journals contains this statement: "Man cannot make principles, he can only discover them. The most formidable weapon against errors of every kind, is Reason[.] I believe that religious duties consist in doing justices, loveing mercy and endeavoring to make our fellow creatures happy."[3]

The secular phraseology seems to be consistent with Enlightenment religious thought, which points to man's association with a larger universe and the interrelationship of the spiritual and the secular in that universe. For the most part, Enlightenment man rejected the emotional fervor associated with orthodox religions. Instead, God appeared as a rational deity who had created the world in an orderly fashion, to be governed by natural laws, and had then removed himself from its affairs. The Enlightenment man fulfilled himself spiritually in his own manner of devoutness by seeking God's natural order in the physical universe through observation and application of natural science and history.

No element of Enlightenment thought is more crucial to understanding Clark's life, expecially his association with Jeffersonian programs, than is the notion of the total interrelationship of all earthly matters. This pertained to worldly objects and creatures as well as to their activities. On a physical plane, this natural order began with the inorganic, progressed to plants and animals, and rose to man and eventually to God in a Great Chain of Being. Understandably, the Enlightenment man expressed an inherent curiosity about his association with past civilizations and other races as well as with contemporary civilizations because he believed that all mankind evolved from one universal body, differing only in the stages of development. The significance of this belief not only instilled in the Enlightenment man a respect for other civilizations, but also fostered an inherent awareness that his personal actions and interests were interrelated with those of the society and nation-state in which he lived. Hence the abstract and the overt, the spiritual and the secular were indistinguishably linked in the Enlightenment world view. As Ernst Cassirer put it,

Philosophy . . . is no special field of knowledge situated beside or above the principles of natural science, of law and government, etc., but rather the all-comprehensive medium in which such principles are formulated, developed, and founded. Philosophy is no longer to be separated from science, history, jurisprudence, and politics; it is rather to be the atmosphere in which they can exist and be effective. Philosophy is no longer the isolated substance of the intellect in its true function, in the specific character of its investigations and inquiries, its methods and essential cognitive process. Accordingly, all these philosophical concepts and problems, which the eighteenth century simply took over from the past, move into new positions and undergo a characteristic change of meaning. They are transformed from fixed and finished forms into active forces, from bare results into imperatives.[4]

Clark's inherent Enlightenment background emerged, not in philosophical terms, but in his role in the implementation of Jeffersonian programs. Clark's career as a Jeffersonian public servant cannot be understood clearly unless it is seen from the Enlightenment perspective of the interrelationship of all of life's components and unless the value of reason and science in unveiling the secrets of that interrelationship is kept in mind. Indeed, Clark's whole life demonstrates a link between public interest and personal interest, between intellectual pursuits of an academic nature and business pursuits. Clark's role in the Lewis and Clark expedition provides an opportunity to see this affiliation of life's components as perceived in the Enlightenment scheme. The expedition provided an intellectual opportunity for a man who, from boyhood, had demonstrated a deep interest in natural science and history. Clark made innumerable scientific contributions to the expedition, many usually attributed to his partner, Meriwether Lewis. In later years, Clark led fossil excavations in Big Bones Lick, Kentucky, and established a private museum in St. Louis, where he displayed specimens and artifacts of the plant, animal, and Indian life of the western portion of the continent.

Clark's association with the expedition must also be viewed in light of its potential for personal economic gain. This cannot be fully understood outside the context of both Enlightenment thought and mercantile capitalism, for the latter also embodied the idea of the interrelationship of individual and national interests.[5] Says one historian of mercantilism: "The state and the individual each had its functions to fulfill. They were both equally in the service of a third, the latter being the 'community.' This vitally important concept was thought of as the common interest of all the inhabitants of a particular social unit, which was not bound to any state or corporate organization."[6]

This is not to say that the mercantilist was any less concerned about his personal wealth than were the men of any other generation. It does seem, however, that he functioned in the belief that his individual prosperity depended on, and was directly correlated to, national prosperity.

Within the context of Clark's life, these Enlightenment and mercantile correlations meant that the Louisiana Territory, as a new and unexplored American empire, could provide vast opportunities for national riches and power which, when obtained, would in a residual sense benefit William Clark personally.

During William Clark's administrative career as an Indian agent in the newly acquired domain of Louisiana in the years following the expedition, the same Enlightenment tendency for seeking harmony between individual ambitions and national interests appeared. As a federal administrator, Clark conducted himself in a manner indicative of his overriding concern for national interests, while at the same time he managed to pursue mercantile interests as a member of the St. Louis Missouri Fur Company. He was able to follow this course because his personal ambitions reinforced, or at least did not conflict with, the tenets of his Enlightenment-inspired Jeffersonian life-style. Of course, Jeffersonian Republicanism and mercantile capitalism shared more than similar assumptions on the economic order of society. Both the Jeffersonian Republican and the mercantile capitalist viewed man as rational and as having a potential to do good through training and experience. Both held the assumption of a hierarchical order of society and a notion that some individuals would emerge with superior skills and wisdom to lead others. Both looked beyond the individual to some larger unit, such as the nation or society. Both reflected the cosmopolitan rather than the provincial. The Jeffersonian dealt in universal concepts, while the mercantile capitalist dealt in the markets of the world. Finally, both visualized the western territories of America within a colonial framework.[7]

Although Clark displayed a definite interest in mercantile ventures, his preoccupation with administering Indian policy and territorial politics never allowed him the time to pursue fully his mercantile interests. After Clark's return from the expedition in 1806, Jefferson appointed him Indian agent for virtually all the tribes in the Louisiana Territory. His role in Indian policy from 1807 until the end of the War of 1812 was chiefly that of a diplomat, befitting Jefferson's general program for the western territories and their native inhabitants. As an Indian official during this period, Clark seems to have been guided by two concerns consistent with national policy. First, he was preoccupied with a fear of losing control of the newly purchased Louisiana Territory to British traders because of their influence on the Indian tribes of the region. Second, and related to his first concern, Clark displayed a great deal of anxiety over the state of American trading practices as an obstacle in achieving the Jeffersonian goal of assimilating the Indian.

After the War of 1812, Clark's role in Indian affairs became increasingly associated with Indian removal. He felt that, owing to the crush of westward expansion, removal offered the Indian a last chance to become assimilated without the corrupting influence of white civilization. The continuing influence of the Enlightenment notion of the interrelationship of earthly components may be seen in Clark's administration of Indian policy. In the mechanistic manner in which Enlightenment man viewed the world, Indian assimilation could be achieved simply by altering the Indians' environment so that it corresponded with that of the yeoman farmer.

At the time of Clark's involvement with Missouri territorial politics, from 1813 to 1820, the gradual erosion of Enlightenment-inspired notions of economic and political order was beginning. As governor of the Missouri Territory, Clark put into practice essentially Jeffersonian notions of government and leadership at a time when the nation and Missouri were entering a new era, an era that jealously guarded individual rights and local autonomy in the face of more nationally oriented programs.

Clark, meanwhile, did not change, nor was he ever able to identify with the new order. The fact that Clark carried out older, Jeffersonian notions of government in the face of the maturing new order caused him to be misunderstood and despised by a great number of Missourians and resulted, finally, in his political defeat in the first state gubernatorial election of 1820. Clark's political career provides a clear contrast between values that guided the old order and those that directed the new. While the frontier man was state making, William Clark was administering a colony. While the frontier man was forming a new society, Clark was manning a colonial outpost. In the old order, Clark was in the vanguard; in the new order, he was an anachronism. From the time of his political defeat in 1820 until his death in 1838, Clark served as the superintendent of Indian affairs in St. Louis, a position that allowed him to remain what he had been since his youth, a product of the eighteenth-century Enlightenment.

II

The Early Years

Wilicliam Clark late in life, as a beleagured public servant, frequently sought refuge from the
pressures of his duties by going to a farm he had
purchased in the countryside surrounding St. Louis. On
a visit to Clark's retreat, Washington Irving captured its
atmosphere of abundant flowering fragrant shrubs which
bordered an orchard "bending and breaking with loads of
fruit—negroes with tables under trees preparing meals—
fine sitting in the open air—little negroes whispering and
laughing."[2] John Flagg, a nineteenth-century traveler,
described the house as a small, white cottage

surrounded by its handsome grounds, and gardens, and
glittering fishponds, partially shrouded by the broad
leaved catalpa, the willow, the acacia, and other ornamen-
tal trees, (which) presents, perhaps, the rarest instance of
natural beauty adorned by refined taste. A visit to this
delightful spot during my stay in St. Louis informed me
of the fact that within as well as abroad, the hand of educa-
tion and refinement had not been idle. Paintings, busts,
medallions, Indian curiosities, &c. &c., tastefully arranged
around the walls and shelves of an elegant library, pre-
sented a feast to the visitor as rare in the Far West as it is
agreeable to a cultivated mind.[3]

11

These images conjure up a picture of genteel refinement tucked away in the Missouri frontier of 1832, and, more significantly, they indicate how much Clark remained a captive of his native Caroline County, Virginia, where he was born August 1, 1770.

Clark's country retreat reflects not only the strong influence of an Enlightenment man and his fondness for nature, but also the flare of a country gentleman reminiscent of a more urbane time and place. Throughout Clark's life on the frontier there are strong indications that he never really considered himself a part of its heritage, preferring instead to look upon himself as an appointed official manning a government outpost. He missed the finer elements of a well-structured Virginia society that he could have enjoyed as a member of one of her leading families. In 1814 he wrote to his brother Edmund in a tone that reflects the thoughts of an individual away only on extended duty. "My friends have to soon forgotten me, do tell me if any cause has assigned for ther not writing. . . . I have plans of living at home someday near you and have a few thousand dollars which I intend to invest in either stock or property."[4] It was more than mere coincidence that Clark returned to Virginia to seek out a wife. In 1808, Clark's quest ended with his marriage to Julia Hancock, a woman whose family had deep roots in Virginia's illustrious heritage.[5] If the physical trappings of Clark's lifestyle seemed "to the visitor as rare in the Far West as it is agreeable to a cultivated mind," it was but an overt indication that William Clark's intellectual makeup stood in stark contrast to that of the Missouri frontier. To begin to piece together the ingredients that shaped Clark's world view, it is essential to look at the environment of his boyhood years. During those years three factors seem to have had the greatest influence on William Clark: the Revolutionary War; a particularly close attachment to his older brother, George Rogers Clark; and the plantation environs of colonial Virginia.

Tradition holds that the Clark family came to the New World in the seventeenth century and settled on the James River in King and Queen County, Virginia. Succeeding generations continued the family occupation of tobacco planting in other parts of the colony. William Clark's father, John III, married Ann Rogers, his second cousin, in 1749 and shortly thereafter moved to a 410-acre estate in Albemarle County on the Rivanna River, part of an inheritance from his father. It was here that four of William's brothers and sisters were born. The Clarks resided in Albemarle County until around 1757, when they moved to a larger and better-located estate on the eastern slopes of the Alleghenies in Caroline County. It was here that the remaining six Clark children were born.[6]

The plantation environs of Clark's Virginia were a mixture of English traditions and New World conditions. Virginia plantation owners resembled English country gentlemen in many direct ways. The overt appearance of their lives contained the similar aristocratic amenities of polite conversation, graceful dancing, and a concern for temperance in all aspects of conduct. Yet despite these similarities, the New World society was more fluid with birth not a guarantee of everlasting genteel living. On the other hand, a frugal yeoman farmer could conceivably enter the upper class by increasing his holdings and emulating the country gentleman's life-style.[7]

Eighteenth-century Virginia social structure was fluid, while still elitist at its core. The New World aristocracy was not based on blood, but on individual achievement and conduct. The Clark family had its roots deep in Virginia and was counted as among the social elite. The

Clarks listed some of Virginia's most respected families among their friends, including the Byrds, the Washingtons, and the Randolphs. In Albemarle County the Clark home was located only one mile from the Jefferson plantation, which helped George Rogers Clark and Thomas Jefferson to become especially close friends.[8] The manner and conduct of the Clark family was totally consistent with that of the Virginia gentry. William's older brother, Jonathan, recalled in his diary dances attended by men in satin coats and lace ruffles plus fox chases, cockfights, and shooting tournaments.[9]

The life-style of the Virginia gentry on educational matters emphasized a broadly based curriculum which consisted of Greek, Latin, classic literature, philosophy, medicine, and history.[10] The older Clark boys, Jonathan and George Rogers, received such an education from the noted Scottish educator, Donald Robertson, who was also Mrs. Clark's brother-in-law.[11] In addition to the Clark boys, Robertson listed as his students such distinguished individuals as John Taylor of Caroline County and James Madison. The latter reportedly said of Robertson, "All that I have been in life I owe to that man."[12] Robertson, himself a product of the Scottish Common Sense school, perpetuated his Enlightenment beliefs to his students personally and through his library, which contained a good mixture of such Enlightenment writers as Locke, Hume, Diderot, Montesquieu, Voltaire, and Montaigne.[13]

Because his family moved to the Kentucky wilderness when he was only thirteen, Clark never received the classical education of his older brothers. He did a remarkable job of becoming self-educated, however, and he benefitted from the education of Jonathan and George Rogers. George Rogers Clark had the greatest impact on William's intellectual development. The older brother held a deep interest in natural history and science, a trait that was so prevalent in Clark's intellectual makeup. George Rogers fondly said of himself: "I don't suppose there is a person living that knows the Geography and Natural History of the back Cuntrey [sic] better if so well as I do myself. . . . It has been my study for many years."[14]

Clark's self-education is of interest because while he demonstrated an intellectual curiosity for a variety of disciplines, he could never write without grammatical and spelling errors because of the lack of formal training. On one occasion, while writing on the importance of geometry, trigonometry, astronomy, navigation, architecture, and land surveying, he seemed to de-emphasize the importance of the form of writing. "Learning does not consist in the knowledge of languages," he said, "but in the knowledge of things to which language gives names. Science and Philosophy."[15] Whether this is simply rationalization for his inability to write well or whether it reflects a deep-seated belief is difficult to assess. The fragment "Science and Philosophy" at the end of Clark's sentence, however, serves as an additional reminder of the equation between scientific inquiry and social progress.

Natural order and harmony in nature was implicit in this world view. The order and harmony that existed in the universe, however, was not always apparent and needed to be closely observed and tested. Progress, therefore, was directly dependent on the number of individuals who were actively seeking to uncover the secrets of the universe. American education and knowledge from all over the world was held in high priority with the government assisting it just as knowledge would eventually assist government in achieving its goals of national and social progress.[16]

The economic and political order prevailing during

Clark's boyhood days in Virginia posited a strong inter-relationship between proper social ethics and intellectual development and economic success. Property ownership was, in other words, synonymous with responsibility and judiciousness as personal characteristics. It is understandable, therefore, why the propertied individual constituted not only the social elite, but also the political elite of colonial Virginia. Consistent with this belief was the notion that only the most responsible, or propertied, citizens should participate in the political process, and of this group only the most judicious should actually hold public office. For this reason, a property qualification accompanied the franchise. The propertied individual, through his economic status, demonstrated personal attributes of superior character, and, because of his status, he had a stake in the interests of the community. In choosing the most judicious man for a position of leadership, the electorate was, in principle, placing in the hands of the ruler the responsibility to rise above the petty interests of specific segments of society and rule on behalf of the entire community. Thomas Jefferson, in his later years, would refer to these gifted individuals as the natural aristocracy. Underlying this early Virginian world view was the assumption that all men were not created equal but that they should have equal opportunity to demonstrate their abilities to their fullest potential.[17] The economic, political, and social order to which Clark was exposed in his early years is important to remember, for it became a part of his intellectual outlook as a Jeffersonian Republican and contributed immensely to our understanding of his views on the administration of Indian policy and territorial politics.

The Revolutionary War was another early influence on Clark's life. He saw five of his brothers go off to fight the

British when he was at the impressionable age of six. The war years were a mixture of pride and tragedy for William. One of his brothers, John, died of tuberculosis while a prisoner on a British ship; the other Clark boys survived the war. Both Jonathan and George Rogers distinguished themselves during the war. Jonathan received a gold medal and a special letter of commendation from General George Washington. The contribution of George Rogers Clark, of course, is more well known. During the Revolution, he was in large part responsible for securing the Ohio Valley for the colonial cause.[18] After the war, the Continental Congress gave him a standing ovation for his efforts, and Benjamin Franklin declared, "Young man, you have given an empire to the Republic."[19] That these events made a deep impression on William was evidenced in later life when he once recalled past events for an audience of admiring nieces and nephews. As one of them remembers, "He was modest in recounting his own great achievement but told with pardonable pride about those of his famous brother, George Rogers Clark."[20]

Several lingering traits in Clark's later years can perhaps be traced to his boyhood impressions of the Revolutionary War. Six-year-old William was impressed by the glorious aspects of soldiering. He demonstrated an eagerness to pursue a military career and, as shall be seen, took advantage of his first opportunity to enlist. More significantly, Clark carried with him to his death a consistent hatred and distrust for the British, a trait which is difficult to point to without recalling the impact of the war years on him.

After the Revolutionary War, the Clark family turned its attention to Kentucky, a territory with which George Rogers had become so familiar during the war. Kentucky was a part of the new "empire" secured by him for the re-

Mulberry Hill, just south of Louisville, Kentucky, the home of John Clark, the father of William Clark *(Courtesy The Filson Club)*

public, and it offered vast new opportunities for him and his family. In 1784 the Clarks migrated to a new homestead south of Louisville which they named Mulberry Hill.[21] Although Kentucky was a wilderness compared to Caroline County, Virginia, the Clark family continued to live as landed gentry. Their home became a social gathering point for the other planters as well as for members of a professional class beginning to form in Louisville. In these surroundings, Clark's boyhood impressions of the British and military life were reinforced, owing to the historical circumstances of the late eighteenth century in the Ohio Valley.

The treaty in 1783 which ended the American War of Independence did not end the diplomatic maneuvering on the part of the French, the Spanish, and especially the British to secure territory in the North American continent. English diplomacy was aimed at the retention of a number of military outposts along the Canadian border, contrary to the peace treaty. Moreover, Britain was interested in the fur trade. The British justified their interest in the posts by indicating that the Americans had not lived up to a provision in the treaty of 1783 which allowed merchants who remained loyal to the British to recover their debts after the war.

Because the new republic of the United States was so loosely organized under the Articles of Confederation, Congress had no power to coerce individual states to comply with the provision in the treaty questioned by the British. Hence, the British retained their posts in the Northwest and their contracts with the tribes in that region, causing an uneasy situation for those Americans inhabiting the Ohio Valley during the last two decades of the eighteenth century.[22]

As the Clarks moved into their new home south of Louisville, British and Canadian officials were busily organizing a confederation of Iroquois, Wyandot, Shawnee, Delaware, Miami, Ottawa, Chippewa, and Potawatomi Indians which was pledged to cede no more land to the United States. If the British had been able to realize such a confederation, the result would have been an Indian buffer state with the Ohio River as its southern boundary. Circumstances were such, however, that a combination of American expansion and disagreement among the tribes concerning boundary lines created a situation ripe for warfare.[23]

This situation led William Clark and his fellow citizens of the Ohio Valley to fear and distrust the British and their contacts with the Indians. This fear was amplified by the isolation that the citizens felt when they were informed by the state government in Richmond that they could expect little help from the federal government if war began. Left to themselves and operating under the assumption that the British were instigating the tribes to attack, the Americans began a series of raids on Indian villages north of the Ohio River in the summer of 1788. As the tribes of that region retaliated, the citizens of the Ohio Valley became embroiled in Indian wars that lasted until final victory in the Battle of Fallen Timbers in 1794.

These circumstances only reinforced William Clark's distrust of the British which he had carried with him to the western territory. During the next several years he became actively involved in a military career and served in a variety of campaigns against the Indians of the Ohio Valley.[24] In 1789 he signed up for military duty under Major John Hardin, who was recruiting an expedition to seek out and destroy certain troublesome Wea villages on the Wabash River. The Hardin campaign was little more than a reactionary force to curb the tribes north of the Ohio.[25] Hostilities increased until in 1790 it became apparent that some organized federal military offensive was needed.

Clark was not a part of the first such efforts which took place under the command of General Josiah Harmar and the governor of the Northwest Territory, Arthur St. Clair. Both men failed disastrously in their efforts, not only in futile attempts to curb the Indians, but also in the number of lives and equipment lost. These disasters naturally increased the confidence of the Indians in their plans to restrict white settlement to lands south of the Ohio River.[26]

In response to a new wave of Indian attacks in 1791, General Charles Scott organized another expedition against the tribes north of the Ohio. Clark became an acting lieutenant in Scott's campaign, serving under Scott's second-in-command, Major General James Wilkinson.[27]

The campaign of 1791, like the others before it, proved less than successful in ending Indian depredations. Frustration over the Indian situation in the Ohio Valley led President Washington to increase federal efforts in the area and to put Major General Anthony Wayne in charge of all such activities. Wayne immediately reorganized the command into four sublegions, with Clark, now a commissioned lieutenant, assigned to the fourth.[28] He remained under Wayne's command until his retirement from military life in 1796.

A selective look at Clark's military career in the Ohio Valley from 1789 to 1796 begins to reveal his personality. His duties were divided among engineering assignments (fort construction), intelligence and diplomatic missions, and escorting supply trains through the Ohio Valley.[29] He emitted an aura of responsibility and confidence, judging from the important and delicate nature of the duties assigned to the young officer.

Beginning in 1793, Clark performed a series of suspected intelligence missions in areas south of the Ohio River near territory occupied by the Spanish. These missions, if indeed they were intelligence oriented, operated under the guise of escorting supplies to the Indians.[30]

Perhaps the most important assignment of Clark's early military career came in 1795 when General Wayne sent him on a diplomatic mission to a Spanish fort which had been constructed south of St. Louis on the Mississippi River in violation of the Treaty of San Lorenzo. After Clark had conferred with the Spanish commandant, he concluded that, while in violation of the treaty, the fort offered no immediate threat to the security of the United States. More significantly, Clark gathered on his mission intelligence data on Spanish military forces and armament, including sketches of Fort Chickasaw. Clark's success in meeting with the Spanish and securing information without provoking an incident so impressed Wayne that he included Clark's report in his own dispatches to Washington.[31]

Although Clark received ample reward and praise for his service in the Ohio Valley Indian campaigns, he grew increasingly impatient with the military. An incident that took place in May, 1794, is evidence of his dissatisfaction. Clark was in charge of a packtrain of seven hundred horses carrying supplies desperately needed for the western campaigns. On the trail, Indians attacked and killed all of the forward guard, thus jeopardizing the whole column. But Clark managed to rally his rear guard with such rapidity that only a few of the valuable packhorses were lost.[32] Writing to his brother Jonathan about the incident, the frustrated young officer lamented, "My merit for my dispositions and Officer like conduct in the (mentioned) fray has not been sufficiently rewarded."[33] Clark's display of raw ambition can be better understood if it is remembered that he was under tremendous pressure to measure up to the achievements of his famous older brother. Furthermore, his impatience and impetuous nature was amplified by the manner in which Wayne conducted his campaigns.

Unlike his predecessors, St. Clair and Harmar, Wayne chose to wage a much more deliberate campaign in the Ohio Valley. He proceeded slowly to train his men adequately and construct a system of forts to serve as supply depots as well as defense works. In addition, at the end of the day in the battlefield, Wayne took the precaution to have his men construct log barricades around the temporary encampments and to post all-night guards. These measures necessarily took extra time and effort and were a source of irritation to his soldiers and frustration to young officers like Clark. Perhaps most frustrating of all to Clark was the crumbling discipline among the officers in the face of friction between Wayne and his second-in-command, James Wilkinson. Wilkinson, in addition to acting as a Spanish spy, had been scheming for the overthrow of Wayne so that he himself could take over command. On one occasion he delayed a supply train so that Wayne's plans could not be carried out with the dispatch originally intended. From Clark's perspective, Wayne's campaign stalled at times when it appeared that a more aggressive plan of action would have achieved success. Wilkinson played on such sentiment to attract to himself a group of officers who, while ignorant of his intentions, held similar views of Wayne.[34] Clark was one of these officers. Given Clark's personality, it is easy to see why he attached himself to a more brash and bold leader, Wilkinson.

Clark became more and more critical of Wayne's military tactics. On one occasion when Indians were withdrawing from their villages, Wayne chose not to attack, ignoring the advice of Wilkinson. The frustrated Clark wrote in 1794,

The scheme was perposed & certain Suckcess issued if attempted—Genl. Wilkinson Suggested the plan to the Comdr in Chief, but it was not his plan, nor perhaps his wish to Embrace So probable a means for Ending the War by compelling them to peace—this was not the first occasion or oppertunity which presented its self to our observant Gel—for Some grand Stroke of Enterprise, but the Comdr in Chief rejected all & every of his plans.[35]

Over a period of months, however, Clark's criticism of Wayne gradually decreased, as did his admiration for Wilkinson. This occurred primarily because Wayne's tactics resulted in a decisive victory at Fallen Timbers in 1794, followed by a peace treaty the next year.

Clark's change of heart concerning Wayne failed to alter his intentions of leaving the service. His travels in the Ohio Valley caused him to see the power and influence of commerce and the potential it had in the western territories. As early as 1794, he wrote to his brother Edmund:

I have some intentions of resigning and get into some business in Kentucky or on the Mississippi. My wish is on the Mississippi as I think there is a great opportunity for an extension of the Mississippi trade in that river could a man form valuable connections in New Orleans which I make no doubt could be accomplished particularly at this early period.[36]

Clark conceived of trade as providing more than economic opportunity. In a letter he wrote on the same day expressing his desire to get into business in a "civil capacity," he stated, "I wuld bid adieu to this unthankful unpolish service. I [am] determined to resign and seek for some more honorable imployment for my youthful days."[37] Clark's personality, with its sense of order and efficiency demanding recognizable, tangible results, found the army and its procedures slow and cumbersome. That Clark did not always control all of the factors in a given situation while in the army produced intolerable frustration.

Clark retired from military life in 1796. Beginning with Reuben Gold Thwaites, most of those who have written about him have concluded that he retired for reasons of health. During the Ohio Indian campaigns Clark was indeed ill, as was every other soldier from time to time. After his leave, however, his health and disposition greatly improved, and yet he still persisted in his plans for retirement. As early as 1794 his intentions of going into trade had been clear, and the end of the Indian wars in 1796 provided an excellent opportunity to retire and become involved in private commerce.

Although the Ohio Valley Indian campaigns were but a brief chapter in Clark's life, their impact on him was significant. His experience in the wars, coupled with his intellectual curiosity, broadened his knowledge in regard to the native inhabitants of this country, a characteristic for which he became noted throughout the rest of his life. Most assuredly these years reinforced his fear and distrust of the British, for in the Ohio Valley he witnessed the power of trade and commerce as a diplomatic tool in addressing the tribes of North America. He also saw the potential for mercantile pursuits in the western territories as a source of national and personal prosperity. When Clark left the military in 1796 he was intent on developing himself as a mercantile capitalist. George Rogers again provided inspiration to William because he had been involved in a variety of mercantile activities in the Louisville area which supplied that growing city with goods and supplies. William's first mercantile adventure came in 1799 when he joined in a canal scheme originated by his brother George. The projected canal was to skirt the falls of the Ohio River, beginning at Clarksville, immediately across the river from Louisville, and to extend to a point a mile and a quarter past the falls. A grandiose scheme, it would have involved $150,000 in capital. A company was formed in 1804 to build the canal, but for reasons not known, after a year of planning the scheme was abandoned.[38]

George Rogers Clark, portrait by Matthew Harris Jouett *(Courtesy The Filson Club)*

At this same time, the combination of his father's ill health, his brother's legal problems, and the famed Lewis and Clark expedition intervened to prevent Clark from ever developing his mercantile interests. George Rogers Clark's difficulties stemmed from careless management of finances during the Revolutionary War. He had been authorized to endorse drafts drawn on the state of Virginia. Over a period of six years Clark readily endorsed such drafts and also often extended his own credit, hoping to settle such matters after the war. In addition he did not bother to ask for his military pay during the entire six-year period. In 1782 he returned to Virginia to present to the state auditors a bill for $20,500. This amount included his personal expenditures for goods, clothing, and other supplies for government troops as well as for his own military backpay. Disaster immediately befell him, because Virginia, while not rejecting his claim, kept it in abeyance.[39]

Simultaneously, drafts which had been endorsed by Clark during his campaign began to be presented by western merchants. The state auditors viewed these claims with suspicion because they represented purchases of goods at prices five to nine times higher than those prevailing on the East Coast. Moreover, Virginia had just surrendered its claim to the Northwest Territory and was in the process of negotiating its compensation with the federal government. Virginia apparently no longer considered legal the expenses incurred in defending its former western territory. In 1792, therefore, Virginia finally rejected Clark's claim, although, through the influence of Thomas Jefferson, he received a tract of land in Indiana as compensation for his unpaid military service.[40]

As a result of the Virginia decision, Clark became responsible both for his own drafts and those endorsed on the state of Virginia. Merchants whose drafts were not honored were themselves often overextended in credit and could not absorb the loss. Soon George became plagued with numerous lawsuits from such merchants as well as from speculators who had purchased unpaid drafts from some of the more desperate individuals among them. George thus found himself in a critical situation, unable to help himself. He lost a great deal of land and might have lost more except for the tireless efforts of his brother William. William wrote to his brother Edmund in 1797:

Our bro G's business is in a disagreeable situation three or four heavy suits pending. . . . I have been agreeable to his request, surveying his lands and doing what part of his business I could which I found in a very unfinished situation. . . . I have rode for Bro. Geo in the course of this past year upwards of 3000 miles continually on the pad, attempting to save him. . . .[41]

One of Clark's land claims, consisting of 73,962 acres, lay in an area south of the Tennessee River. As this claim was in Indian Territory, neither George nor William could do much with it, but then again, neither could George's creditors.[42]

In addition to suits stemming from the Revolutionary period, George was plagued at a later time by a lawsuit instituted by a Spanish merchant named Bazadone. He claimed that Clark had illegally confiscated twenty-four thousand dollars worth of goods in 1797 while on an Indian expedition. The suit hinged on Clark's right to confiscate the goods as a military commander. In this case William was able to get the suit dismissed, saving George from further financial disaster.[43]

Since George Rogers Clark felt that he had been dealt an injustice by the state of Virginia, he, in turn, had no compunction against dodging suits being brought against him. William served him well in this situation by paying off recognized debts and, in return, having George's lands signed over to him in order to prevent further confiscation by creditors. William thus took title to seventy-four thousand acres on the Ohio in cancellation of a debt of $2,100 and of fifteen thousand acres representing payment of a debt of L434. Subsequently, George gave William outright ownership of two thousand acres for services during his financial crisis.[44] George could have done little else to help himself, for if he had gone into business, his creditors would have seized his assets.

The Clark family affairs did not improve after John Clark III died in 1799. He left his son George only three slaves because of the danger that he would lose any appreciable inheritance to creditors from the Revolutionary War. And so William received most of the Clark estate, which included twenty-four slaves, a distillery, a grist mill, and 7,040 acres of Kentucky land. In addition, he inherited lands north of the Ohio River which George had signed over to his father.[45] This seemingly gave William Clark a sizable inheritance, but it came to him as a family trust from his father, and he felt a responsibility for handling it. In addition to the estate being burdened with debts, William paid out ten thousand dollars to his brother's debtors, which forced him to sell part of the estate to his older brother Jonathan.[46]

By 1800 the initial crush of lawsuits had subsided enough for William to get away from his family's problems. In the years 1800 and 1801 he spent much time on the East Coast fraternizing with his close friend Meriwether Lewis, whose acquaintance he had made while in the service of Wayne's army. Lewis at that time was in the service of President Jefferson, as his private secretary. Unfortunately, few records remain of Clark's life during the first several years of the nineteenth century. Because of his interest in natural history and science, he had much to talk about with Jefferson, with whom he also shared a close association through George Rogers Clark and an interest in their common Virginia heritage.

Although the family crises were behind Clark for the moment, he was never able to get back to his own business ambitions. On June 19, 1803, he received a letter from his friend Meriwether Lewis inviting him to take part in an expedition to the Pacific Coast.[47] With his acceptance, Clark would enter the arena of public service, never to leave.

In the preceding thirty-three years, Clark had seen the colonies emerge as an independent nation. In Virginia and Kentucky he had seen this new nation threatened by the Indians and the British. He had seen the military from two vantage points. In his childhood and adolescence it had served as the protector and stabilizer of his world. As he became involved in it, he realized how much of himself could not be satisfied in the army. Nevertheless, the military remained in his mind a key instrument in society. His view on the capabilities of the military was qualified, however, for in the early stages of the Indian wars in the Ohio River Valley it had failed to do what the commercial maneuverings of the British traders had achieved. He saw the powerful influence of commerce on the Indians and its role in determining his nation's quest for a position of security and maturity in the world. With the success of the British traders in the Ohio Valley, commerce became, in addition to an "honorable" profession, an influential one in which the results of an individual's toil could be more effective and more immediately recognized. In this view, a trip to the Northwest made sense to William Clark—not just for himself, but for the good of the country.

III

Surveying the Empire

The Lewis and Clark expedition has become the symbol of an age marked by American continental expansion. It has caught the attention of America in much the same manner as man venturing into the unknown has captured the imagination of past civilizations. Unfortunately, interest in the expedition has centered mostly on its episodic aspects. The perils of hostile Indians and uncharted wilderness have proved so fascinating that serious study of some facets of the expedition has been slighted.

Only recently have studies closely examined the scientific objectives of the mission, and even in doing so they have neglected Clark's scientific role. Clark is generally pictured as the rugged and simple frontiersman, skilled in woodsmanship and the ways of the wild. Meriwether Lewis, on the other hand, is depicted as the educated, sophisticated coleader whose profuse and literate observations contributed most to the scientific goals of the expedition.[2]

And though some studies have emphasized the scientific purpose of the mission in general, there still remains the task of considering the relationship of its diplomatic and scientific goals.[3] The historiography of the Lewis and Clark expedition to date reflects an attitude that the scien-

31

tific and diplomatic goals were inconsistent with one another and that, therefore, one or the other must have predominated in the motives of Jefferson. This stems from the conceptual framework of contemporary historians who live in an age when a variety of interests must compete, one against the other, for priority on a lineal scale. Unfortunately, this viewpoint has little chance of revealing the Enlightenment-influenced mind of Jefferson, who did not see society as consisting of interests on a lineal scale but viewed society as a conceptual whole with each of its interests contributing in an interdependent manner to the best interests of the whole. Thus there was consistency between the diplomatic and scientific goals of the mission. A look at the events leading up to the expedition and Clark's role in it will make this point evident.

The territory traversed by the expedition already belonged to the United States; however, this had not been so during the planning stages of the journey. Earliest American concern with the Northwest had focused on the region surrounding the Columbia River, to which both the United States and Great Britain held tenuous claims. Great Britain had been the first to make its influence felt there, a matter which caused great concern to the Americans. As early as 1783, George Rogers Clark received a letter from Thomas Jefferson expressing his concern over British colonial schemes in the Northwest. "They pretend it is only to promote knowledge, I am afraid they have thoughts of colonization into that quarter. Some of us have been talking here in a feeble way of making the attempt to search that country but doubt whether we have enough of that kind of spirit to raise the money."[4]

Jefferson continued to pursue this issue when, as minis-to Paris in 1786, he encouraged an adventurer named John Ledyard to descend the Missouri River from the west to American territory. Ledyard's journey ended abruptly with his arrest by the Russians in Kamchatka, a peninsula on the far northeastern coast of Russia. Jefferson was no doubt pleased when, in 1790, the federal government authorized an expedition to be headed by John Armstrong. This mission proposed to ascend the Missouri River, but it too was halted when the men were turned back by hostile Indians.[5]

Despite these failures, Jefferson did not put aside his fears of the British and their western ventures and his hopes of improving America's position in the Northwest. In 1793, while vice-president of the American Philosophical Association, he proposed yet another expedition to the Pacific to be led by French botanist André Michaux. Jefferson hoped that Michaux could find a water connection between the Missouri River and the Pacific Ocean. The mission, however, stalled in Kentucky because Michaux became involved in the schemes of Edmond Genet. (Genet had been sent by France on a secret mission to seek support among American settlers in the frontier regions for an attack on Spanish territory in the area of the Gulf of Mexico and New Orleans.) As Genet's representative in Kentucky, Michaux became so involved that his upriver expedition suffered delay and, finally, complete abandonment.[6]

The failure of these American-sponsored ventures into the Northwest made it seem likely that Jefferson's fears of British supremacy there would be realized. In 1794, Alexander Mackenzie climaxed two decades of British probes into the Northwest by successfully crossing Canada to the Pacific. Although unsuccessful in his primary objective of finding a usable water route to the Pacific, Mackenzie did lay the basis for further British exploitation of the region. In 1801, in fact, he published his plans for trade and politics in the region under the title of *Voyages from Montreal*. Because of America's concern over Mackenzie's proposals, it is no coincidence that Lewis and Clark carried a copy of this work with them on their voyage to the Pacific.[7] Mackenzie's progress and his published plans for the Northwest perhaps created the atmosphere favorable to Jefferson's hopes. As president of the United States in 1803, he was finally able to find both the "spirit" and the money for a Pacific expedition, and he persuaded Congress to appropriate twenty-five hundred dollars for the venture.[8] The resulting expedition had goals similar to those originally held by Michaux and by the British ventures. Jefferson hoped that his agents would find a usable water route for commercial transport to the Pacific and record scientific observations along the way.

Since the planning of the expedition preceded the Louisiana Purchase of 1803, it was confronted with a diplomatic problem. To meet the primary objective of locating a water route in the Columbia River region, the expedition would have to cross the Louisiana Territory, then owned by Spain. The territory had been ceded to France by Spain, but the actual transfer had not yet taken place. Jefferson, therefore, sought to obtain Spanish permission to send the expedition across Louisiana. He told the Spanish minister that although the intention of the journey was scientific, Congress had no power to appropriate funds for that kind of activity, and, therefore, the expedition would be announced as having the primary objective of exploring the commercial potential of the Northwest. The Spanish offered no obstacle to Jefferson. They had no fear that the Americans would find a usable water route to the Pacific—if indeed that was Jefferson's intention. The Spanish, as well as Mackenzie earlier, had attempted that and had failed.

The acquisition of Louisiana Territory by France created a real diplomatic problem for the Americans. The Spaniards had been passive neighbors and had permitted free navigation of the Mississippi River. Napoleon, on the other hand, had made France into the world's greatest military power, and this could prove a threat to the peaceful status of the United States. The main foreseeable problem for the Americans, then, lay in keeping the Mississippi River open to free navigation, for it was the only real navigable water outlet for the western territories of the United States. At the same time the Americans understood the need to keep the river open without going to war with France. To emerge victorious from such a war, they felt the United States would need to ally itself with British sea power, a situation which America wanted to avoid at all cost.

With such thoughts in mind, Jefferson appointed Robert Livingston to open negotiations for the purchase of New Orleans or, at least, to secure the right to navigate the Mississippi River and to use New Orleans as a port. Livingston returned not only with New Orleans, but with the whole of Louisiana. Napoleon had sold the territory because of a change in military strategy. Rather than attack the British Empire in the Western Hemisphere, he chose to take an offensive on the European continent. With a situation of war between France and England, then, Napoleon wished to deprive the British of such a great prize.[9]

When the news of the Louisiana Purchase was released, the Lewis and Clark expedition was already at the mouth of the Missouri River making final preparations for its ascent. The news altered the objectives of the mission only slightly. It had already been instructed to make scientific observations and to collect information for possible com-

Thomas Jefferson, from the portrait by Mather Brown, London, 1786 *(Courtesy Frick Art Reference Library and Charles Francis Adams),* (From *Thomas Jefferson, American Tourist,* by Edward Dumbauld)

mercial exploitation. With the territory now a part of the United States, a still greater emphasis was placed on the Missouri River. It could serve as a route back to the East as well as the road to the elusive connecting river that would carry America to the Pacific Ocean. Jefferson now spoke in terms of a route to the Atlantic Ocean that would be faster than the northern British route through Montreal. One major object, however, remained the same—to monopolize the fur trade of the Northwest and hence curb British influence in the area.[10]

If anyone questions the importance of the scientific goals to the Lewis and Clark expedition, he need only read the correspondence of President Jefferson to Meriwether Lewis on June 20, 1803. The letter dwelled on the commercial importance of the mission and outlined in detail the geographic and cartographic expectations of the undertaking. The letter went on to list the goals which combined commercial interests with intellectual curiosity.

The commerce which may be carried on with the people inhabiting the line you will pursue, renders a knolege of these people important. you will therefore endeavor to make yourself acquainted, as far as a diligent pursuit of your journey shall admit,
   with the names of the nations & their numbers; the extent & limits of their possessions; their relations with other tribes or nations; their language, traditions, monuments; their ordinary occupations in agriculture, fishing, hunting, war, arts, & the implements for these; their food, clothing, & domestic accomodations; the diseases prevalent among them, & the remedies they use; moral & physical circumstances which distinguish them from the tribes we know;
peculiarities in their laws, customs, & dispositions;

and articles of commerce they may need or furnish, & to what extent.[11]

To this point it can be concluded that Jefferson's interest in the tribes of the Northwest is purely commercial. He went on to state:

> *And considering the interest which every nation has in extending & strengthening the authority of reason & justice among the people around them, it will be useful to acquire what knolege you can of the state of morality, religion, & information among them, as it may better enable those who endeavor to civilize & instruct them, to adapt their measures to the existing notions & practises of those on whom they are to operate.*[12]

Although Jefferson assumed that the best interest of these tribes lay in a Western life-style, he nevertheless exhibited the Enlightenment notion that all civilizations were derived from one universal body, and, therefore, "every nation has [an interest] in extending & strengthening the authority of reason & justice among the people around them. . . ." Beginning from this Enlightenment premise of the common origin of all civilizations, it perhaps can be concluded that the Northwest tribes served not only the commercial interests of the United States, but also a scientific purpose by supplying valuable insights into God's mechanistically organized world and, hence, greater insights into the nature of man and the social system by which he can prosper the most and live in the greatest harmony.

In the Great Chain of Being not only did other civilizations appear valuable to social and political technicians such as Jefferson, but of equal value were all earthly objects that revealed the interrelationship of God's mechanistically related world. In this vein, Jefferson's letter to Lewis went on to stress as goals of the mission observations of

the soil & face of the country, it's growth & vegetable productions; especially those not of the U.S.

The animals of the country generally, & especially those not known in the U.S.

the remains and accounts of any which may be deemed rare or extinct:

the mineral productions of every kind; but more particularly metals, limestone, pit coal & saltpetre; salines & mineral waters, noting the temperature of the last, & such circumstances as may indicate their character.

Volcanic appearances.

climate as characterized by the thermometer, by the proportion of rainy, cloudy & clear days, by lightening, hail, snow, ice, by the access & recess of frost, by the winds prevailing at different seasons, the dates at which particular plants put forth or lose their flowers, or leaf, times of appearance of particular birds, reptiles or insects. [13]

When seen from the precepts of Jefferson's conceptual framework, it seems academic to debate whether the goals of the mission were for conquest, commerce, or science, for all three objects blended indistinguishably into one purpose. If one of the goals of a social and political experimenter is to secure and develop the empire, the commercial motives of the mission cannot be discounted. If at the same time one of the goals of this experiment is to develop a social and political system which is judicious yet also allows its citizens the opportunity to prosper and live in harmony with one another, the scientific goals of the mission cannot be discounted. Such knowledge may lead to insights that could unlock the universal truths, which in turn could lead to more perfect political and social systems.

As further evidence that the Lewis and Clark expedition was not solely a commercial and diplomatic mission, one need only to look at the political debate fostered by the acquisition of the Louisiana Territory. Although the acquisition of the Louisiana Territory had little effect on the objectives of the Lewis and Clark expedition, it did cause the federal government to give consideration to the political problems the acquisition brought with it. It was necessary to determine what the relationship of the new territory would be to the rest of the country. Was the new territory to be considered for potential statehood? Was it desirable to see the territory populated by settlers? How might the region best be utilized to serve American interests and curb British influence in the Northwest? Talk in Washington revealed fears of the territory becoming populated and brought under the influence of Britain and Spain. Jefferson himself conceded that he would discourage settlement until land east of the Mississippi was occupied. Some in Washington went so far as to propose that the purchase be dealt with as conquered territory. The Louisiana Territory eventually came to be treated as a colonial possession with the military acting as its government. It was seen as the domain of the fur trader who would bring the region under American control, thus curbing British colonial schemes.[14]

To lead the expedition, Jefferson turned to Captain Meriwether Lewis, his private secretary and a close family friend. Lewis fulfilled in Jefferson's view the qualifications necessary for such a journey. He was a natural leader and had a knowledge of woodsmanship. In addition, he was capable of scientific training. The selection of a companion was left to Lewis. In making his choice, Lewis looked for a man with a military background who could serve as coleader of the expedition. In addition to possessing the obvious qualifications for this kind of journey, such a man must have the skills of a draftsman in order to make maps of the territory covered. Most important, though, Lewis indicated that he wanted someone to his personal liking. His first choice for such a companion was William Clark, an old friend from the Ohio Valley Indian campaign days.[15] On June 19, 1803, Lewis wrote to Clark proposing that he join the expedition:

. . . you will readily conceive the importance of an early and friendly and intimate acquaintance with the tribes that inhabit that country, that they should be early impressed with a just idea of the rising importance of the U. States and of her friendly dispositions toward them; as also her desire to become useful to them by furnishing them thrugh her citizens with such articles by way of barter as may be desired by them or useful to them—the other objects of this mission are scientific, and of course not less interesting to the U. States than to the world generally. . . .[16]

The aims of the expedition were highly compatible with the notions that Clark held. Clark understood the commercial potential of the western territories, as he had already expressed to his brother in 1794.[17] He was equally aware of the power of commerce, having witnessed the influence of the British traders during the Indian raids in the Ohio Valley. Furthermore, he had expressed his interest in the sciences, and the prospects of the new and the unknown titillated his imagination. Not surprisingly, then, Clark answered Lewis' letter two days after he had received it. "My friend I join with you hand and Heart and anticipate advantages which will certainly derive from the accomplishment of so vast—Hazardous & fatiguing enterprise."[18]

The venture was organized under military regulation. While Lewis held the rank of captain, Clark was recommissioned only as a first Lieutenant because of bureaucratic procedures which neither Lewis nor Clark had the time to correct. The two, despite the difference in their rank, looked upon each other as equal in command. Evidence of this is the fact that Clark was referred to as "Captain Clark" throughout the journey.

Lewis and his party got under way at Pittsburgh on August 31, 1803, and moved down the Ohio River to Louisville, Kentucky, where they met William Clark, his slave York, and a number of volunteers recruited by Clark. Together the party journeyed to the mouth of the Missouri River, where they wintered in final preparation for the ascent of the river. The next May the expedition, consisting of forty-five men, set off in three boats, two pirouges, and a fifty-five-foot keelboat. By November, 1804, they had arrived in what is presently North Dakota, where they wintered among the friendly Mandan Indians. The spring of 1805 saw the party leave the Mandans minus sixteen men who had been sent back to St. Louis with some early reports and specimens of the journey.[19]

The party did pick up one member, a Shoshone girl, Sacagawea, who had been held prisoner by the Mandans. The girl was the wife of one of the expedition's interpreters, Toussaint Charbonneau, the latter having won her in a gambling session. Sacagawea has become famous as a scout for the Lewis and Clark expedition. In fact, however, she served only in a limited capacity as a guide. She was, though, very helpful to the expedition as an interpreter of unfamiliar dialects once the party had reached the Rocky Mountain tribes.[20]

After leaving the Mandans, the expedition journeyed as far as the Great Falls of the Missouri River in what is presently Montana. There the party moved westward over the Continental Divide, reaching the mouth of the Columbia River by early winter of the same year. By Christmas the party had settled in its winter quarters known as Fort Clatsop. The expedition began its return journey the following spring in late March of 1806. Three months later the expedition split into two parties for exploratory purposes. They later rejoined at the confluence of the Yellowstone and Missouri rivers and continued downstream, arriving in St. Louis on September 23, 1806.[21]

If historians have failed to deal effectively with the motivations of the Lewis and Clark expedition, they have also failed in relating the comparative roles of each of its coleaders. The writing of Reuben Gold Thwaites more than that of any other historian seems to have cast the two main characters into personality molds that have been accepted ever since.

Thwaites, in 1904 and 1905, was the first to edit comprehensively the journals of the Lewis and Clark expedition. The two earlier major editions by Nicholas Biddle in 1814 and Elliott Coues in 1893 were at best incomplete versions. In addition to Thwaites' discussion of the personalities of Lewis and Clark in the introduction to his comprehensive edition of their journals, he followed in 1906 with an article specifically about Clark entitled: "William Clark: Soldier, Explorer, Statesman." The article implies that Thwaites conceived of William Clark as a child of the frontier, well versed in its coarse and wild ways, who

matured into a soldier and later a statesman well equipped
to serve his country on the frontier. Thwaites contrasted
Lewis and Clark quite succinctly, but, with thought, still
broader implications become apparent. He described
Lewis as a "philosophical man who loved flowers and
animals," while Clark was "less educated, writing brief
and pointed comments."[22] Bernard DeVoto, perhaps the
most imaginative of all those who have written about the
expedition, seems to have followed the stereotypes popu-
larized by Thwaites. He sees Lewis as the "diplomatic"
and "commercial thinker," while Clark was the "negoti-
ator." Lewis was the "scientific specialist," and Clark was
the "engineer and geographer as well as the master of
frontier crafts." Lewis was a sensitive man with a "speculative mind" subject to changing moods, whereas Clark
was "even tempered" and, through implication, less sensitive.[23]

Thus both Thwaites and DeVoto gave the impression
that Lewis was the "intellectual," performing those tasks
which required thought and reflection. Clark, on the other
hand, is fondly pictured as a man of unusual physical
skill and adeptness in the ways of the wilderness. Recalling
Clark's life up to then and looking at his performance on
the expedition, a slightly different Clark emerges. It can
be said that Clark was as much of a "diplomatic and commercial thinker" as Lewis. For example, in writing to
George Rogers Clark in 1806, William Clark underscored
his concern with commercial factors and their political
implications:

*I consider this tract across the continent of immense ad-
vantage to the fur trade, as all the furs collected in 9/10
parts of the most valuable fur country in America may be
conveyed to the mouth of the Columbia and shiped thence*

to the East Indies by the 1 of August in each year and will
of course reach Canton earlyer than the furs which are an-
nually exported from Montreal in Great Britain.[24]

Recalling Clark's earlier interest in trading on the Mississippi, the potential for trade on the Upper Missouri
must surely have stirred his imagination. On the return
trip to St. Louis in 1806, Clark wrote to Toussaint Charbonneau: ". . . if you wish to return to trade with the
indians . . . I will assist you with merchandise for the purpose and become my self concerned with you in trade on
a small scale that is to say not exceeding a perogue load at
one time. . . ."[25]

Commentators on the expedition have accepted Lewis
as the "scientific specialist" trained in botany, zoology,
and celestial navigation. The journals indicate that Clark
made a much more significant scientific contribution to
the Lewis and Clark expedition than heretofore thought.
A study completed on the linguistic contributions of Lewis
and Clark underlines Clark's contribution to natural history. It comments on Clark's vocabulary by indicating
that, "It may be said that he is responsible for several
natural history terms applied to the new animals of the
west. . . . There are many good examples. But he used
none of the scientific adjectives so common with Lewis. . . ."[26]

The fact that Lewis was better versed in scientific jargon
and that most of the journal entries were in Lewis' hand
because of his obviously superior writing qualities has
possibly misled historians into overstressing the scientific
contributions of Lewis and largely ignoring those of Clark.
This should not be misconstrued as an attempt to mini-
mize the role of Lewis in the expedition. Indeed, he was
specifically trained for the scientific aspects of the mission,
while Clark was not. However, one cannot discount Clark's

boyhood interest and achievements in the fields of natural history and science. In addition, there are other scientific achievements that can be attributed to Clark. For example, Lewis was trained to take most of the celestial readings and, indeed, the journals indicate he did. Clark, though, was not ignorant of the techniques for taking celestial readings. In addition to several entries which indicate this fact, Clark carried with him a notebook containing five problems in celestial navigation and examples for their solution.[27] Furthermore, Clark was recognized as being in charge of much of the navigational data, a task that requires a knowledge of trigonometry. Clark also made almost all of the geographical sketches and observations. The maps that he brought back with him are, to the present time, considered remarkable in their accuracy and quality.

There is also a case to be made for Clark's ethnographic contributions to the expedition. Consider Clark's observations of the Pishquow Indians, just one of many made during his lifetime.

This Tribe can raise about 350 men their Dress are Similar to those at the fork except their robes are smaller and do not reach lower than the waste 3/4 of them have scercely any robes at all, the women have only a Small pece of a robe which covers their Sholders neck and reaching down behind to their wastes, with a tite piece of leather about the waste, the brests are large and hang down verry low illy Shaped, high Cheeks flattened heads, & have but fiew orniments, they are all employed in fishing and drying fish of which they have great quantities on their scaffolds, their habits customs &c. I could not lern.[28]

In addition, consider his detached and objective view of the sexual mores of the Chinooks.

An old woman & Wife to a Cheif of the Chunnooks came and made a Camp near ours. She brought with her 6 young Squars (her daughters & nieces) I believe for the purpose of Gratifying the passions of the men of our party and receving for those indulgiences Such Small [presents] as She (the old woman) thought proper to accept of.

Those people appear to View Sensuality as a Necessary evel, and do not appear to abhor it as a Crime in the un-married State. The young females are fond of the attention of our men and appear to meet the sincere approbation of their friends and connections, for thus obtaining their favours, the Womin of the Chinnook Nation have hansom faces low and badly made with large legs & thighs which are generally Swelled from a Stopage of the circulation in the feet (which are Small) by maney Strands of Beeds or curious Strings which are drawn tight around the leg above the ankle, their legs are also picked [i.e., tattooed] with defferent figures. . . .[29]

If Clark was simply the rugged frontiersman he is pictured to be, it seems unlikely that following the expedition Jefferson would have entrusted him with leading a party to Big Bones Lick, Kentucky, in 1807 for the purpose of excavating fossils. Clark was very successful in excavating the fossils of Pleistocene mammals, gathering some three hundred specimens.[30] A grateful Jefferson wrote Clark,

[I] am greatly religed [sic] indeed by the trouble you have been so good as to take in procurring for me as through a supplement to the bones of the Mammoth as can nor be had. . . . The collection you have made is so considerable that it has suggested an idea I had not before. I see that after taking out for the Philosophical society every thing they shall desire there will remain such a collection of

duplicates as will be a grateful offering from me to the National Institute of France. . . .[31]

It might be said that Jefferson chose Clark not because of the latter's interest in natural science and history but because he was a dependable and able leader of men. If this is the case, then it seems that Jefferson would not have taken the trouble to inform Clark later about one of the fossils he had procured. Regarding a bone which Clark felt was that of an elephant, Jefferson indicated that it was instead "a distinctive kind to which they [the National Institute of France] have given the name of Mastodont. . . ." Jefferson went on to describe some of its characteristics. He conjectured that they were meat eaters because "nature seems not to have provided other sufficient for him; and the limb of a tree would be no more to him than a bough of cotton tree to a horse."[32]

Further evidence of Clark's interest in natural history and science comes in a letter he wrote to Jefferson in 1825 expressing an interest in the University of Virginia, which had just been founded, and offering to assist in providing artifacts for the museum of natural history at that institution. He wrote:

As one of the objects of the institution . . . is the collection of a Museum of natural history of minerals & Curiosities in general of and on nature; it would afford me pleasure to contribute Something towrds it of such articles as are sometimes collected in this Western Section of the Union. . . .[33]

As a government official residing in St. Louis at a later point in his life, Clark took upon himself the task of establishing his own museum of natural history. His collection, while dominated by "Indian curiosities," also contained a large number of animal and reptile skins, mineral samples, and bones of extinct prehistoric mammals, including those of the mastodon. The Indian curiosities consisted mostly of headdresses and other articles of clothing, hunting, and war implements, such as the bow and arrow and the battle axe, and a large birchbark canoe.[34] On the quality of Clark's achievement and museum, Henry Rowe Schoolcraft, a noted author and traveler, wrote:

He evinces a philosophical taste in the preservation of many subjects in natural history, together with specimens of Indian workmanship, and other objects of curiosity, collected on the expedition; all of which are arranged with considerable effect, in the building occupied as a council-house for the St. Louis agency. We believe this is the only collection of specimens of art and nature west of Cincinnati, which partakes of the character of a museum, or cabinet of natural history.[35]

Many travelers visiting the territory took time to go through Clark's museum. Perhaps the most famous visitor was the American Revolutionary War hero General Marquis de Lafayette, who returned to America for a visit. While in St. Louis, Lafayette took time to visit with William Clark and to see his museum. On this occasion possibly the two men spoke of Clark sending to France articles pertaining to the natural history of America. Several years later, Clark, in grand fashion, had a live grizzly bear sent to General Lafayette in France. Lafayette's response to the gift must have pleased Clark immensely:

The grisely [sic] Bear you Had the goodness to send me, Has been more admired on this side of the Atlantic, as it was the first animal of the kind, living or dead, that Had ever made its appearance in Europe. I was inclined to make a pet of Him as He was then very gentle. But it was thought wiser to put Him under the care of the Board of Professors at the jardin des plantes, *the fine European Museum of Natural Philosophy.*[36]

Thomas Jefferson, General Lafayette, and the French were not the only ones who appreciated Clark's scientific interest. In 1838, after Clark's death, the Academy of Natural Science passed a resolution eulogizing him for his scientific merits. As a token of their loss, the members wore crepe on their left arms for thirty days.[37] Such tributes to Clark expand our understanding of him far beyond that of the buckskin-clad, Indian-wise wilderness creature depicted by Reuben Gold Thwaites.

It is difficult to explain why Thwaites presented Lewis and Clark as the "intellectual" and the "backwoodsman," respectively, when there was considerable evidence to the contrary. It is significant, however, that Thwaites was much more fascinated with William Clark than he was with Meriwether Lewis. This may have been due to the time in which Thwaites was writing. The early twentieth century saw historians beginning to come to grips with a census report of 1890 that declared the frontier gone for all time, followed in 1893 by Frederick Jackson Turner's provocative frontier hypothesis. These events seem to signal the close of an era, an era to which Thwaites had devoted his professional career. He perhaps looked nostalgically upon Clark as one of those frontiersmen who did so much to further the greatness of America, one whose values were rapidly being altered by the industrial consciousness of the time. In such a mood Clark represented a dying breed of rugged individuals. Lewis, on the other hand, held no such fascination for Thwaites because Lewis was generally associated with Jefferson, whom he served as private secretary, and with the East and the intellectual and cultural refinement usually attached to it.

The Lewis and Clark expedition, although failing in one of its primary objectives—finding a usable water route to the Pacific—can be considered a success. Bernard De-Voto suggested that "success in a strange country required a curious mixture of open-mindedness and skepticism capable of adjusting accepted ideas and practices to unfamiliar conditions."[38] These qualities in both men perhaps emanated from their being born close to the values of the eighteenth-century Enlightenment which rejected tradition and encouraged a natural curiosity and, at the same time, a healthy respect for customs foreign to them.

William Clark proved especially adept in dealing with the tribes and thereby displayed traits that had characterized his life to that time. He became known to the Indians as a firm, honest, and judicious man.[39] Until his death Clark's reputation among the Indians caused him to be besieged constantly with requests for mediation, counsel, and assistance in all matters. The bond of trust established by Clark, however, was slowly eroded by American traders and trading practices, in addition to the westward push of civilization.

The expedition served further to solidify Clark's image as viewed by others. It amplified on a national level his reputation as a dependable administrator with a personal demeanor well suited for dealing with people, red and white. Thus Clark became valuable not only to the federal government, but to the fur trade, to the future Missouri Territory, and perhaps most of all, to the Indian. From this time until his death Clark would remain a public servant.

The expedition had failed to locate a Northwest passage and to confirm the feasibility of capturing the Canadian fur trade. It did pave the way for the exploitation of the beaver. It also underlined the fears of British penetration in the upper Missouri, a matter that would preoccupy Clark's mind and, consequently, his actions for the rest of his life.

"Commerce is the great engine by which we are to coerce them. . . ."[1]

Jeffersonian Indian Policy

S afely back from the Pacific, William Clark accompanied Meriwether Lewis to Washington to give a full report of their journey. In addition to presenting their findings, both men anticipated receiving payment for their participation in the expedition. Each of the coleaders received $1,228 and sixteen hundred acres of land for their services. Jefferson also showed his appreciation by offering both men public offices of considerable responsibility. He appointed Meriwether Lewis as governor of the Louisiana Territory and made William Clark the Indian agent for the tribes of that territory and brigadier general of the Louisiana Militia.[2] These appointments were not merely rewards for, in Jefferson's mind, conditions and circumstances in Louisiana demanded dependable and loyal public servants.

The security of the Louisiana Territory appeared to be threatened by external forces from Britain and Spain, as well as by internal intrigues from the Burr faction. After completing his term as vice-president under Jefferson, Aaron Burr saw himself as politically and financially bankrupt in the East as a consequence of his duel with Alexander Hamilton. But because of his ambitions, Burr looked to the recently acquired Louisiana Territory for new opportunities. Two factors aroused his fancy. He saw that the French inhabitants of Louisiana were unhappy under American rule. He was also aware of a boundary dispute between Spain and the United States that could possibly lead to war.

Though never found guilty for plotting such a scheme, Burr allegedly hoped to unite the discontented elements in the West and form an independent empire with New Orleans as its capital. Burr enlisted an old hand at intrigues, James Wilkinson, to aid him in this adventure. Wilkinson had been appointed military governor of Louisiana in 1805 and thus held an ideal position from which to launch an attack on Mexico in the event of a war with Spain. If such a war occurred, Burr supposedly hoped to take a group of volunteers and, with the help of the British, capture New Orleans. His plans began to fail, however, when Britain showed no interest in his scheme. In addition, Wilkinson realized that Burr's plans had become widely known and decided to betray him by calling Jefferson's attention to the scheme. When Burr realized that the federal government had been alerted, he surrendered to American officials in 1807. James Wilkinson was discredited because of his role in the affair and, while not court-martialed, was assigned new duties in the Northeast, far removed from the arena of the alleged intrigues.[3]

The discrediting of Burr and Wilkinson removed only a part of the threat to the newly acquired American empire, for there was still an economic war to be waged against the British and the Spanish if the Louisiana Territory was truly to become a part of the American domain. It was in this arena that Jefferson sought help from two friends who had recently done such a creditable job for him—Lewis and Clark. As governor of the Louisiana Territory and Indian agent respectively, Lewis and Clark served as key diplomatic officials in implementing Jeffersonian programs for the western territories. The major source of discontent in Louisiana, as seen through Jefferson's eyes, was the fur trade. Intense competition existed among American traders as well as between American trading interests and those of Britain and Spain. Hence, the first priority of Jefferson's program which concerned William Clark was the organization of a territorial militia and regulation of American fur-trading practices. Simultaneously, fur-trading interests were to be directed so they might serve national interests in the most beneficial manner.

Jefferson remained suspicious of private traders operating under the existing system and attributed to them the causes of Indian unrest. He hoped to rid the western territory of the bothersome influence of private trading interests by underselling them in trade and forcing them into some other endeavor more useful to the country. Jefferson hoped to achieve this end by extending a system of government trading posts, known as factories, west of the Mississippi River.[4]

The "factory system" had been officially instituted under President George Washington in 1796. Strained relations between the United States, Great Britain, and Spain had an influence in obtaining congressional approval of government ventures in business. Aside from the French, British, and Spanish trade policies, there were also earlier American precedents for such a practice. In 1775 the Continental Congress appointed a committee to formulate a program for official trade with the Indians. Later, President Washington saw the need to draft more precise plans for procuring goods and for holding the allegiance of the American Indian. In 1795, Congress debated a fifty-thousand-dollar appropriation for the purchase of goods to be traded to the Indians at special sites chosen by the federal government. On May 18, 1796, Congress finally passed such a bill, specifying that government-owned trade goods would be handled by government-appointed "factors" at designated posts or factories. The factory system was to be terminated at the end of two years unless extended by congressional action. Though renewed every two years thereafter, congressional interest in the system gradually declined.

In 1806, however, Jefferson aroused new interest in the system by proposing to extend its scope and uses.[5] In his mind the system could serve as the key diplomatic and economic weapon for protecting American interests in the western territories. He wrote to Meriwether Lewis, "Commerce is the great engine by which we are to coerce them [the Indians], and not war."[6]

It is impossible to understand Clark's role in Jeffersonian Indian policy without first understanding the conceptual base of the program he implemented and influenced over the years by his advice to national officials. To understand Jeffersonian Indian policy, it is necessary to consider the dictates of the American Enlightenment with the provisions of that policy. Jefferson viewed the Indian as a member like himself of the universal body of man. He considered Indian and American cultures as essentially part of one universal civilization, the two differing simply because environmental circumstances had caused the Indian to remain at a more elementary stage. Hinging the development of civilization on environmental factors posed a problem to the Enlightenment thinker in considering the prospects of improvement not only for the Indian, but also for American civilization. Benjamin Barton, a noted eighteenth-century naturalist, argued that Indian civilization could be improved:

... the physical differences between nations are but incon-

siderable, and history informs us, that civilization has been constantly preceded by barbarity and rudeness. . . . The Americans are not, as some writers have supposed specifically different from the Persians, and other improved nations of Asia. The inference from this discovery is interesting and important. We learn that the Americans are susceptible of improvement.[7]

Hence, "Indian" society, like "American" society, was viewed as a stage of civilization. Unlike his contemporaries who attributed an inferiority of the Indian to a life-style incompatible with American civilization, Jefferson instead pointed to the savage environment of the Indian and his well-developed faculties for wilderness living. The Indian, according to his reasoning, displayed a lack of talent for American living only because he had no occasion to be confronted by its environmental dictates.[8] On this subject he wrote to the French naturalist Chastellux in 1785:

. . . I am safe in affirming that the proofs of genius given by the Indian of N. America, place them on a level with Whites in the uncultivated state. . . . As to their bodily strength, their manners rendering disgraceful to labour, those muscles employed in labour will be weaker with them than with the European labourer: but those which are exerted in the chase and those faculties which are employed in the tracing an enemy or a wild beast in contriving ambuscades for him, and in carrying them through their execution, are much stronger than with us, because they are more exercised. I believe the Indian then to be in body and mind equal to the white man.[9]

According to this logic, if the environmental trappings of the Indian were made similar to those of the white

American, the Indian would emerge eventually into the same stage of civilization currently occupied by the rest of the Americans. If the Indian could be persuaded, even coerced, to surrender his huge tracts of hunting land in favor of ownership of smaller agricultural tracts, the assimilation of the Indian, in Jefferson's mind, would be a scientific certainty. This is in stark contrast to the prevalent historical interpretation which stresses the primacy of economic self-interest in American Indian policy.[10]

Jefferson placed as much stress on economic motives as does this traditional interpretation, making one subtle distinction. From Jefferson's mercantile Enlightenment perspective, individual components of society, because of their relationship, could not prosper without the whole societal unit prospering. This idea contrasts with the contemporary notion that the whole societal unit prospers only when individual rights are protected.

Seen from this perspective, a whole new light is cast on Jefferson's land-acquisition policy and the function of the factory system.[11] In Jefferson's mind the factory system could serve as a key diplomatic and economic weapon for protecting American interests in the recently purchased Territory of Louisiana, as well as a device for assimilating the Indian. American national interests, hence, would be achieved through this system because Indian allegiance to the British and Spanish interests would be diminished. Simultaneously, Indian reliance on huge tracts of land would be lessened, thus accelerating his assimilation into American life.[12] In this context Jefferson even felt justified in advising William Henry Harrison, governor of the Northwest Territory, to encourage the Indians to accumulate large debts at the various factory posts, making it necessary for them to sell their land. Thereby they would face the necessary stimulation to become assimilated into

American life or to remove themselves west of the Mississippi, where in time they would achieve the common destiny of progress for all members of the human race.[13]

Jefferson was not dealing in hopes and dreams when he attempted to change the Indians' environment from a hunting to an agricultural stage. His concepts rested on scientific "facts" forged into his own thinking from the finest Enlightenment minds of his age—John Locke, Francis Bacon, Isaac Newton, Lord Kames, David Hume, and Denis Diderot, men who were as unquestioned in eighteenth-century America as Albert Einstein was in the fourth and fifth decades of the twentieth century. It was not a question of whether the Indian might assimilate but a question of how soon he would assimilate, and institutions such as the factory were seen as vehicles for bringing about this scientific inevitability.

Conceiving of a program was one thing, actually gaining its acceptance was quite another. Jefferson proceeded cautiously, for he was dealing with a nation which had just freed itself from a mother country viewed as trampling on American rights through excessive government regulation. Considering this atmosphere, Jefferson expected that his program of expanded government business ventures and trade regulation involving factories spread all the way to the Pacific Ocean would not be easily accepted. Mindful of this, in 1803, Jefferson asked only for a renewal of the existing factory system. But in the same year he also began a three-year campaign to prepare Congress for a program of expanded government involvement in territorial economic matters.

By 1806, of course, Lewis and Clark had returned from their journey and had given Jefferson a full report of their findings. They confirmed Jefferson's suspicions about the degree of British penetration in the Northwest and the feasibility of carrying on a profitable trade in that region. Lewis and Clark also reported that they had obtained promises from the tribes of the upper Missouri to trade in American factories which were to be established.[14]

Armed with such information, Jefferson became convinced more than ever of the value of the fur trade in securing Louisiana for American national interests. The scene was set for him to move ahead with his program. He still, however, needed congressional approval. Indian trade regulation was one matter, but to drive out private trading interests would be a difficult task to accomplish. In his congressional message of 1806, Jefferson reported those findings of the Lewis and Clark expedition that were of diplomatic interest. This information and his own three years of patient cultivation of Congress were enough to persuade that body to extend the factory system west of the Mississippi. Congress authorized the establishment of twelve new factories, and, while no mention was made of it, Jefferson felt he was on his way to controlling Louisiana and maintaining peace among the Indians by excluding private trading interests.[15]

Jefferson's plans never matured to their final stage, nor did they need to. Only three of the twelve proposed factories were established west of the Mississippi for the purpose of trading with the Indians. The first post was built in 1805 at Bellefontaine, just above the mouth of the Missouri River at St. Louis. In 1808, Fort Madison was built in southwest Iowa and Fort Osage just east of present-day Kansas City.[16] The bill which established the factory system also provided for the appointment of a superintendent of Indian trade to be responsible for purchasing and distributing goods to the factories. The superintendent as well as the factories were under the direct supervision of the secretary of the treasury. The initial capital appropriated for the system was $260,000, including a $10,000 annual outlay for salaries of clerks and factors.[17]

In 1807, when William Clark began his duties as Indian agent in St. Louis, he stood enthusiastically in the vanguard as implementor of those programs. Viewing Clark's early association with Indian affairs through the day-to-day workings of his office is not as important as seeing his practical application of the Jeffersonian ideals discussed earlier. Clark's role as an Indian official seems to have been guided by three concerns consistent with national policy. First and foremost he became preoccupied with a fear of losing control of the newly purchased Louisiana Territory to British traders because of their influence on the Indian tribes of that region. Second, and interrelated with the first concern, Clark displayed great anxiety about the chaotic state of American trading practices and the irregular nature of American trading regulations. Finally, because of the nature of the Burr conspiracy and internal dissension, Clark reorganized the military, excluding any factions sympathetic to Burr or others of his persuasion.

Clark revoked all existing commissions and made new appointments with individuals he deemed loyal to national interests. Appalled at weaknesses in the militia, he reported to the secretary of war that:

The Militia (when organized) was so scattered that they will afford but a feeble defence to extensive frontiers of this Territory against the Indians. Their numbers, I believe to be about Two thousand four hundred effective men. To prevent the probability of an Indian [attack] (Which can only be effected by Spanish *or* British *influence and intreague) it will in my opinion be necessary to have some establishments of troops in the Indian Country; as well to watch the embisarys of those Nations;*

*as to inforce the laws regulating the intercourse with the
Indian tribes &c.*[18]

The military reorganized and staffed with loyal officers,
Clark's next concern was American trading practices and
the danger presented by the influence of foreign traders
on the Indians. To this end he enthusiastically agreed
with Jefferson's assessment of the problem. In 1808 he
wrote the secretary of war:

*The maney abuses which has crept into the habits of the
Indian Trade, and the unfair practices of the white
hunters, on the Indians hunting Lands has been a just
cause of complaint; and induced me to establish certain
regulations to be observed [which] . . . I flatter myself
correct these abuses, and bring more friendship sistem
and order, and the Indian of that quarter will be more
under the eye of the U State Agents.*[19]

In an earlier communique Clark revealed exactly what
he felt was harmful about American trading practices.
"The great variety of interests conceived in the Indian
Trade of this Country and the irregular method which
they have caried it on, is calculated to give the Indians an
unfavorable opinion of the American regulations."[20] Implicit in Clark's statement is a belief that the source of the
problem lay in the "variety of interests" and that the matter could be resolved only through government regulation
and government-sponsored business ventures. Clark
carried this belief with him throughout the remainder of
his life. Later in life he advocated a government monopoly
in the fur trade at a time when western settlers were extremely adamant about obtaining more freedom for private enterprise.

Part of Clark's concern over the "variety of interests" in the fur trade was that smaller trading parties would not be effective competitors against the powerful British North West Company because the latter had a monopoly granted by the British government. The logical conclusion of this development meant that the tribes of the Northwest would remain loyal to the British and, hence, the Louisiana Territory would not be truly an integral part of the American domain. Clark indicated this concern clearly when he wrote of the North West Fur Company "This association appears to be calculated to injure this Country very much[.] all the rich furs and peltries with which this Territory abounds will fall into the hands of British Merchents."[21] Attributing the word *calculated* to the acts of the British was tantamount to stating that Britain was at war with United States—an economic war, but nevertheless war. This closely represented Clark's sentiments at the time. In Clark's mind he was the vanguard of his nation's struggle for security. As further evidence of this, five months later Clark referred to the British in even more threatening terms when he stated that "the conduct of the British traders in the northwest is such as cannot be put up with by our government."[22]

As an Indian official of the national government, Clark thus saw his duty not so much as solely promoting the specific interests of the inhabitants of the trans-Mississippi West, but in retaining that vast region to serve national interests and thereby serving the interests of the private trader and the American Indian. In retrospect this seems an impossible goal to achieve, but from Clark's world view it was obvious and necessary for national development.

Clark's dealings with the Osage Indians provide an example of how the Jeffersonian mind saw conflicting interests as interdependent. There had been frequent complaints by settlers that the Osages were stealing horses from them. Clark confronted the chiefs and elders of the Great and Little Osage. They seemed, in microcosm, to epitomize for him what had been happening in the Indian country. The chiefs explained that only a few of their people were given to stealing from the white man and that they felt a whole people should not be punished for the actions of a few.[23] Previous punishment of the Osages, however, had extended beyond the trials of a few individuals and provided seeming justification for white men and other Indian tribes to invade and occupy their hunting grounds.

Clark considered the plight of the Osages in light of what he already knew about illicit trading habits, including the dangerous effects of intoxicating liquor, and he undoubtedly felt a deep compassion for them. Compassion, interpreted in Clark's framework, meant securing the interest of the United States in the western territories while at the same time attempting to adjust the life-style of the Indian in a manner more compatible with current national developments. In a plan consistent with Jeffersonian Indian policy, Clark attempted to persuade the Indian to live an agrarian life and to depend on the government factories for necessary goods. The Indian, thus able to make himself comfortable in this mode of living, would no longer need large tracts of land.

Clark's treaty with the Osages clearly demonstrated these principles. According to its terms, the Osages placed their protection in the hands of the United States while relinquishing land amounting to two-thirds of the present state of Missouri and one-half of the present state of Arkansas.[24] From a contemporary frame of mind the relinquishment of so much land by the Indians can be seen as yet another example of a "land grab" by the white man.

If for a moment, however, one were to take seriously Jeffersonian beliefs that the Indian really would become a yeoman farmer with red skin were his environment altered, then Clark's treaty with the Osages is seen from a new perspective.

To assist in the cultural transfer that would inevitably occur, Clark promised the Osages "to keep a Store at that place to trade with them, to furnish them with a Blacksmith, A mill, Plows, to build them two houses of logs, and to pay for the Horses and property they have taken from the citizens of the U. States since the accession of Louisiana."[25] To curb the "maney abuses" in the Indian trade, Clark proposed greater regulation and supervision. While government regulation of the Indian trade had long been an established practice, Clark realized that the trans-Mississippi Indian country presented new problems. In an area where Indians still held large tracts of land, much confusion existed over boundaries and the jurisdictional applicability of trade regulations. In a methodical and orderly manner, therefore, Clark began to clarify boundaries and, in addition, demanded that trading take place only in places of defined American jurisdiction. He decreed that all traders operate within the confines of the fort and under the supervision of government officials. In addition, no traders could hunt on Indian lands.[26]

Another facet of Clark's solution involved an increase in personnel. He recognized the vastness of the Indian country and could foresee no alternative but to increase the number of administrative and military personnel.

Clark also took steps to control Indian activity within the western territories as a diplomatic factor in the economic struggle between the United States and Great Britain. With tensions between these two nations running high, the citizens of Louisiana felt apprehensive for their safety. The spring of 1809 was a particularly tense time, made even more so by the lack both of regular communication with the East and of information on international developments. Isolated, the citizens of the western territories momentarily expected war with Great Britain. If that should happen, western officials such as Clark firmly believed that settlers in that part of the country would bear the brunt of a British-inspired Indian attack. Because of inadequate defenses for so vast an area, Clark became especially wary of the movements of Indian tribes. For that reason he employed an intelligence network consisting of Indian subagents, military officers stationed at outposts, friendly Indians, and spies to keep him informed of the Indian situation.[27] Through his intelligence network he became convinced that the British had incited the Shawnee leader the Prophet to plan an attack in the spring of 1809. Evidence of this intention seemed clear in the massing of tribes in the Illinois Territory. On the basis of such evidence, Clark organized the whole territory in a state of defense by constructing additional fortifications and mustering additional militia units. In 1809 the great gathering of tribes began to break up, and it appeared as if the danger had passed. Though no clear evidence remains of plans for such an attack, Clark personally believed that it had been planned and that the Indians had been discouraged by the show of force which the Americans mustered.[28] This incident only contributed to the crisis mentality that Clark brought to his tasks in the territory. It was these concerns coupled with conceptions of a paternalistic government regulating society for the common good that guided Clark's public and private actions in other territorial matters as well, affairs that already in 1807 showed signs of strain between federal territorial programs and the interests of the settlers.

V

Securing the Empire: The Merging of Public and Private Interests

W hen Louisiana Territory was turned over to the United States, Jefferson signed a law that divided the area for administrative purposes. That region south of the thirty-third parallel beginning at the Mississippi River and extending to the western boundary of the territory became the Territory of Orleans. This congressional action so disturbed the residents in the northern District of Louisiana that they protested through a petition the law which subordinated them to the government of the Indiana Territory. In addition, the Spanish land-grant situation caused uncertainty among the residents in Louisiana because of the time-consuming and complicated Spanish method of confirming land titles. The system required that the settler submit a petition to the regional commandant who, in turn, ordered a survey of the claimed lands. Then the information was sent to officials in New Orleans for final approval. This last arduous step was seldom taken prior to the American takeover, and, consequently, the opportunity was created for land speculators intent of fraud to seek large acreages.[2]

Some residents of the troubled territory petitioned Congress to nullify all Spanish land grants made after the territory had been ceded back from Spain to France. They also protested the transfer of Indians from east of the Mis-

sissippi into their territory, an action that naturally com-
pounded local problems of defense and increased the fears
of residents for their safety. Most important, petitioners
asked for a territorial status of the second rank. This, in
essence, meant a resident government consisting of a governor and an elected assembly. Congress, for the most part,
ignored petitioners, but it did establish upper Louisiana
as a territory of the first rank. Though less than had been
requested, this did provide for an appointed governor to
reside in the territory and for three appointed judges to
act as a legislature. The laws of this territorial government
were also subject to veto by Congress.[3]

Although the transfer of the Louisiana Territory to the
United States had been peaceful enough, a struggle between French and American settlers for political dom-
inance was inevitable. William Clark's political career
ultimately became embroiled in this struggle. Immediately
after the transfer of the territory, however, the wealth and
economic power of the region rested mostly with the entrenched French families, such as Auguste Chouteau's.
The French appeared to have taken the transfer quite
well, and they emerged with their influence intact. Their
leaders as a whole accepted roles of responsibility in the
American system. Between 1804 and 1816, for example,
Auguste Chouteau accepted an appointment as a presiding
judge, became colonel of a regiment in the militia, served
as president of the St. Louis Board of Trustees, and became
president of the first organized bank in St. Louis.[4]

Remembrances concerning St. Louis in its earliest days
under American ownership express a note of congenial-
ity between the French and American cultures. Henry
Brackenridge attributed to the Americans a spirit of enterprise and industry which was passed on to the French,
while the latter contributed gentility to the common man-

ners of the Americans. In a similar vein, Margaret Hunter Hall recalled that the women of St. Louis were generally noted as being the most tasteful in their dress and manners. She also indicated that the leaders of St. Louis were the most cosmopolitan and cultured in the West.[5]

Such a spirit and tone in St. Louis society did not last. "By the end of the third decade of American rule, most of the French looked on helplessly while they were being absorbed and overwhelmed by the more numerous, wrangling, covetous, liberty-loving, equality-demanding Americans."[6] This element of Louisiana society which represented the new order was already clamoring for a more representative relationship with the federal government when Clark arrived in 1807. From the perspective of his own life, Clark no doubt sympathized with such demands, but he also recognized the need to keep the territory under tight control because of the danger presented by Britain and Spain. The new settlers viewed the territory less from the focus of its foreign implications than in terms of their own self-interest. From their view it seemed unreasonable to have eastern Indians transferred to their vicinity and outrageous that no truly representative territorial government existed.

A letter to the editor of the *Missouri Gazette* in February of 1819 contained a verse expressing an attitude that, in decades to come, would prevail in Missouri and in the nation:

Thine, Freedom, thine the blessings pictured here
Thine are those charms that dazzle and endear;
while ev'n the peasant boas'st these rights to scan
And learns to venerate himself as man.
While self-dependent power can time defy
as rocks resist the billows and the sky.[7]

The letter also criticized the newspaper for not publishing petitions seeking a second-rank government. It ended by stating, "To govern and be governed are distinct things; the one is supremacy, the other obedience."[8]

In 1807 the Louisiana Territory, and particularly St. Louis, remained primarily dependent on the fur trade and lead mining for economic livelihood. Before the Lewis and Clark expedition, a limited fur trade had been dominated by three men, Auguste and Pierre Chouteau and Jacques Clamorgan. With the opening of the upper Missouri and the entrance into St. Louis of the enterprising Manuel Lisa, the fur trade was extended not only geographically, but it also now included new members.

The government's approach to the lead-mining industry and to the fur trade was similar. It was felt that a tight rein had to be kept on affairs in Louisiana and that included its mines. Moses Austin, a Virginia miner who came to Louisiana to take advantage of the lead mines, reported to Jefferson that existing policy did not serve the public good. Austin stated that in his opinion the mines were government property and should not be worked by individuals without taxation. Accordingly, in 1807 the federal government adopted a leasing system which served as the basis for government policy until 1846, when a new world view interpreted what the basis of the relationship between private enterprise and government should be. In essence the leasing system stated that all mining lands not then in private hands would be retained by the government and leased to individuals for not more than five years. Later, in 1807, the leasing system was further clarified to include a royalty on ore taken from the mines, as well as a reduction of the lease period to three years.[9]

Although upper Louisiana was not besieged by settlers until after the War of 1812, St. Louis, the economic hub of

upper Louisiana, was already, in the first decade of the
nineteenth century, bustling with new merchants moving
in to do business alongside established French firms.
Limited housing and high rents were not the only problems these merchants faced. Specie was so scarce that one
traveler declared, "I do not believe that I assert too much
though it may be surprising to you in saying that the entire business of these waters is conducted without the use
of money."[10]

The scarcity of money and an agricultural way of life
for the new settlers forced merchants to extend long-term
credit. A general optimism about the territory's future
made the credit system work until the panic of 1819 dis-
rupted the economy. Before that, much land passed from
one owner to another as a result of defaults on debts.[11]
St. Louis, despite its growth and activity, had difficulty
establishing itself as a wholesaling center before the 1830's.
Even then, prices in St. Louis were 15 to 20 per cent higher
than in the East Coast centers of Philadelphia and Baltimore.[12]

Western merchants, however, did capitalize on the fur
trade, primarily by supplying foodstuffs and last-minute
needs for fur-trading expeditions.[13] Western merchants
also participated in government trade operations by bidding for the hides and furs marketed by the government
factories and, later, by bidding for contracts to supply
annuities for migrating Indian tribes.[14]

Clark was well acquainted with the economic conditions
in Louisiana during the first decades of American control
because, in addition to being a government agent in a diplomatic and administrative capacity, he also served as an
economic agent. In 1808 he accepted the additional responsibility of receiving and disposing of goods traded at
the two recently established factories in his jurisdiction.[15]

To make Clark's job more delicate, he was faced with enforcing the Embargo Act of 1807. The United States was caught between British and French antagonism in the years from 1804 to 1807. American ships were constantly intercepted by British ships in search of contraband. American seamen were also removed from their ships and pressed into British service. In response to the general outcry of Americans against this practice, Jefferson imposed an embargo on British goods as a means of peaceful coercion. Clark enforced the embargo with strict disregard for local interests. For example, a friend, Christian Wilt, consulted Clark about obtaining some goods through British auspices. Clark responded with a warning that all British goods could be seized under the embargo.[16] The restlessness of local merchants toward government policies was reflected in a letter from the territorial secretary of war. "The merchants complain of restrictions beyond the Provisions of the Law; of arbitrary regulations established without a motive and relinquished without a reason and of various other irregularities by which their commerce has suffered a damage. . . ."[17]

While rigid in enforcing government policy, Clark did co-operate with local merchants for their benefit when it was in the interest of the government. Christian Wilt approached Clark with a scheme for setting up a string of barges between St. Louis and Pittsburgh. Clark encouraged Wilt by promising him a share of the transportation of government goods.[18] Communication and economic links with the East made sense to a man charged with securing the colonial frontier. In the economic war that was being waged in the western territories between the United States, Great Britain, and France, the foot soldier was replaced by the mercantile capitalist, be he government agent or private trader.

In this economic sphere William Clark became involved through personal business interests. Though most of his energies were still devoted to public service, he became engaged in several ventures, the most ambitious of which was his association with the Missouri Fur Company.

While Clark was one of its organizing fathers in 1809, the Missouri Fur Company owed its existence to a crafty and resourceful Spaniard named Manuel Lisa. Lisa was born in New Orleans and developed into a seasoned trader before coming to St. Louis in 1798. In only three years he became one of the leading traders in St. Louis, a remarkable achievement since his competitors there had dominated the Indian trade through monopolies granted by Spain.

After failing to persuade Spanish officials to take a free-trade approach to the St. Louis area, Lisa managed to entice the Spanish to grant him a monopoly already held by another merchant, but which was about to expire. Lisa prospered in St. Louis and was not disturbed, like some of his colleagues, when it was announced that Louisiana was being transferred back to France, possibly to be sold to the United States. The fact that the Americans would open trade to all who wished to compete suited Lisa fine; after all, he had attempted earlier to get the Spaniards to do the same thing.

An ambitious man, Lisa felt that the largest possible fortune would be found in the distant trade regions of either the Northwest or the Southwest.[19] The return of the Lewis and Clark expedition immediately prompted Lisa to involve himself in larger and more ambitious ventures. As his first joint venture he joined forces with two established Illinois merchants, William Morrison and Pierre Menard. This partnership, which had a capital investment of $16,000, was the first organized trading venture to travel up the Missouri River to the Rocky Mountains. The party left in the spring of 1807 and, after little more than a year in the field, returned safely back to St. Louis in the summer of 1808. The three partners each received $2,667.50 in furs, with Lisa getting an additional $985.00 for leading the expedition.[20] More important than the details of this venture was the effect it had on the St. Louis merchants. Because Lisa had demonstrated that one could pass through hostile Indian country unscathed and return with an appreciable quantity of furs, the St. Louis-based traders now had to decide whether they wanted to compete for the upper Missouri fur trade.

Besides competing with one another, the St. Louis traders had to consider the powerful British North West Company, already entrenched in the Northwest, and the American Fur Company, which was operating at that time in the Great Lakes region but which would conceivably move west in a matter of time. Another factor to be considered was the change in American policy toward Indian trading.[21]

The Americans had been in possession of Louisiana for only three years before reports from frontier officials, especially Meriwether Lewis, somewhat altered Jefferson's previous plans for securing that region. From Lewis' reports, which no doubt were influenced by Clark, Jefferson eventually adopted two distinct policies toward the Indian trade. Lewis believed that the traders in the vicinity of the American frontier should be encouraged in fair competition but held to trading only at designated posts under the supervision of government officials. On the other hand, he felt that St. Louis merchants would shy away from competition with the powerful North West Company under such government restrictions. For that reason Lewis proposed a separate policy for trade on the upper

Missouri. He first advocated a government-owned company, but, realizing that this was not feasible, he proposed a policy that removed all restrictions from traders going into that region.[22]

With restrictions now removed, Lisa, Menard, and Morrison were spurred on with thoughts of a large venture in the upper Missouri fur trade. To achieve this, however, more capital was needed, and so meetings were held with other merchants during the winter of 1808–09 with a view towards forming some sort of temporary joint trading association. Out of these meetings emerged the association known as the St. Louis Missouri Fur Company. As the region in which it was founded ultimately became the Territory of Missouri, the company was eventually referred to as the Missouri Fur Company.

The founding members were Benjamin Wilkinson, Pierre Chouteau, Sr., Manuel Lisa, Auguste Chouteau, Jr., Reuben Lewis, William Clark, Sylvestre Labbadie, Pierre Menard, William Morrison, and Andrew Henry.[23] The members came from diverse backgrounds. Wilkinson, Morrison, Menard, and, of course, the Chouteaus were all established merchants. Labbadie was a wealthy and educated landowner who dabbled in trade. Reuben Lewis was employed by the government as a subagent for the Osage Indians. Andrew Henry, a man of little wealth who had previously been associated with mining in Missouri, invested most of his assets in the fur venture and was perhaps included for the services he could perform as a field captain.[24]

Clark was included because he could add to the success of the organization in several ways. As a government agent for Indian trade, he was in regular contact with the secretary of war concerning the marketability of government furs. Through correspondence with Secretary of

Five members of the
Missouri Fur Trading Company:
top left, William Clark;
top right, Manuel Lisa;
middle left, Sylvestre Labbadie;
middle right, Pierre Chouteau;
bottom, Auguste Chouteau

War John Mason, the two men exchanged information necessary to enable them to make the wisest decisions in purchasing goods for the agency and disposing of government furs. In 1808, typical of this correspondence, Clark wrote:

I received at this place a fiew days ago, a fiew Indians presents directed to me and forwarded from Pittsburgh. Several articles wet & damaged. the freight of those articles as also the Sac Annuities, I was obliged to pay very high for. — Would it not be cheaper and more convenient to the government to send all Stores *intended for this place to Fort Masac and boats sent from this place to Fort Masac for stores — men are always to be precured here at 20 and 25 dollars a trip and found — . One Small and one large Boat would be sufficient for this Service — I think I could engage some of the merchants of this Country or Louisvulle to receive the stores at Pittsburg or Wheeling and deliver them at Fort Masac, much lower than those have been brought on laterly to that place.* [25]

On another occasion in 1809, Clark wrote to the secretary of war, "Inclosed is a list of such articles as can't be percured here on better terms than in the Seea port towns of the U.S. . . ."[26] In turn the secretary's letters to Clark included advice on the disposal of government furs. In August of 1809, Mason told Clark that while New Orleans was usually the best market for deerskins, it now was unfavorable. He therefore instructed Clark to store the skins until spring, when, it was hoped, conditions would improve.[27]

Through his government contacts, Clark was undoubtedly the best informed man in St. Louis on the conditions of the fur market. In addition, because of his experiences on the Lewis and Clark expedition, Clark could add prestige to the organization and provide invaluable information on the geography, the inhabitants, and the navigational problems within the intended trade area.

Clark was enthusiastic about the Missouri Fur Company because of its potential role in fulfilling national policies. The venture, if successful, could potentially cut into the strong hold that the British North West Fur Company had on the Northwest fur trade and, hence, greatly enhance American commercial interests in that region.

The Articles of Agreement of the Missouri Fur Company called for every member to share equally in expenses of the fur-trading expedition. Each member was also obligated to accompany the major expedition or send a representative. The articles also bound members to do everything in their power for the benefit of the entire company. Each member was prohibited from trading separately for furs with any group or party for individual profit. The company agreed to purchase all its goods, supplies, and horses from the previous Lisa-Menard-Morrison organization. The members also agreed that, upon arriving at the point of the Mandan village on the Missouri River, each partner would either proceed with the expedition or reside at posts designated by the majority of the membership under the penalty of a one-thousand-dollar fine.[28]

The articles went on to make specific designations for various members. Manuel Lisa and Benjamin Wilkinson were selected to do the actual trading with the Indians encountered. No merchandise was to be purchased without the consent of the majority of the partners. When purchases were approved, William Clark and Pierre Chouteau were "appointed and fully authorized by the Company to sign and execute all notes, bills, obligations, receipts discharges & acquittances for and in behalf of the Company."[29] The articles provided detailed instructions outlining which members would return to St. Louis and in what order. Pierre Chouteau, Manuel Lisa, and Pierre Menard would return to St. Louis the first year, and Benjamin Wilkinson and Auguste Choteau would return the next. The men of both groups were to return to the field by the next spring or be subject to a forfeiture of five hundred dollars. The furs sent downriver were to be disposed of as quickly as possible and the profits divided equally, with shares being available on demand rather than at a set date. This rather cautious provision indicated, perhaps, that the partners were suspicious of one another and consequently wanted the freedom to take their share of the profit at any time they wished. Likewise, at the end of the three-year term of association, all property was to be divided equally among the members. With this agreement consummated on March 7, 1809, the Missouri Fur Company was launched.[30]

The finances of the company were strengthened through a contract with Governor Lewis to return a Mandan chief, Shahaka, to his village. This agreement specified a sum of seven thousand dollars for the return of the chief if the voyage to his home territory began before April 20, 1809, and if not begun before May 10, the company would forfeit three thousand dollars of the original fee. Lewis added still another reward for prompt service. He promised to license no other traders above the Platte River before the last date stipulated for the departure.[31] The federal government later rebuked Lewis for making such a generous contract for the return of the Mandan chief.[32]

The optimism felt by members of the Missouri Fur Company soon dissipated, for almost from the departure of the main body in June, 1809, the expedition, consisting of 210 men, was plagued by setbacks. The rigid military discipline imposed by the company, especially Lisa, resulted in the desertion of many employees before the expedition even reached Fort Osage. Desertion took its toll to the point that Lisa wrote to Clark from the fort informing him that a boat, a pirogue, and supplies were being sent back to St. Louis to be sold for the company's benefit.[33] From the start, however, the company must have been overequipped. Several weeks before the main party departed, Clark placed an advertisement in the *Missouri Gazette* offering for sale a quantity of supplies, including ammunition, guns, and tobacco.[34]

The troubles of the company continued. When the partners reached the Mandan village, they learned that the British North West Company had erected a fort near the Three Forks of the Missouri. Coupled with this news of British entrenchment came word that the Blackfeet Indians of that region had driven out most of the private trading groups who had ventured there.[35] News of the abundance of furs, however, spurred the company on despite the odds against success.

The company continued to build posts at suitable points along the route. At one of these, Cedar Island, located below the Mandan village, the partners suffered their most severe loss. The post burned to the ground, resulting in the loss of furs estimated to be worth between twelve and fifteen thousand dollars.[36] To add to this disaster, upon returning in succession to St. Louis, the partners learned that an embargo on British goods had been imposed, closing off the foreign fur market and consequently glutting the domestic market and depressing the price of beaver. At the end of its first year of operation, with two parties led by Andrew Henry and Reuben Lewis still in the field, the company realized only a slight profit and then only because of the revenue obtained by the return of the Mandan chief and the sale of surplus goods.[37]

In addition to its financial problems, the company quickly developed a questionable reputation. A rival party led by Ramsay Crooks and Robert McClellan had to turn back from an upriver trading expedition because the Sioux nation expressed great hostility. Since it was known that a party led by Manuel Lisa had successfully gotten past the Sioux shortly before, traders in St. Louis suspected the Missouri Fur Company, and especially Lisa, of encouraging the Sioux to oppose Crooks and McClellan. The federal government, too, was unhappy with the company for charging Lewis so much for the return of Shahaka.

In the winter of 1809–10, Clark went to Washington to explain the company's position on the Shahaka affair and to improve its image in the eyes of federal officials. In a letter to Pierre Chouteau, Clark reported that his visit seemed to improve the government's outlook on the company, especially after he explained the foreign implications of its activities.[38] Here again it might be said that Clark chose to influence the federal officials primarily because of his own interests in the Missouri Fur Company. To be sure, Clark was interested in personal gain, but it must be understood that from his perception of matters, no distinction existed between personal and national gain when the two proved compatible. Clark's total experience, his Enlightenment upbringing, his close association with Jefferson's programs, and his obsession with the British traders as a menace to American goals— all contributed to his willingness to seek governmental approval for the company's program. Shortly after his return from Washington, Clark again expressed concern over British trading interests. "I fear that the British Traders in the N West will compele all the American hunters & Traders to abandon that eminately rich Country of which they had taken great Possession without interference or protection of the Gen. government."[39]

Indeed, government support, while still present, was not as enthusiastic as it had once been. On March 4, 1809, a new president, James Madison, was inaugurated, and, while he allowed the current Indian program, of which the factory system was the most crucial part, to continue, he never exerted much personal influence on its behalf.[40] Congress continued to extend the life of the factory system, but it no longer played a key role in national plans. Because of increasing tensions with Great Britain, Washington officials began to stress the problems of the eastern and northeastern sections of the country, a trend that became pronounced during the War of 1812.

Meanwhile, it became clear to the partners in the Missouri Fur Company that the embargo and their own series of financial setbacks would necessitate some reorganization. In a meeting held September 10, 1810, the stockholders voted to send a party to aid Henry and Lewis who were still upriver. They appointed Lewis, Menard, and Clark to organize that mission, with total expenditures not to exceed $6,750 for men and goods.[41] In addition, the partners made some organizational changes based on their first year's experiences. They agreed that thereafter only two members of the company needed to go upriver at any one time and that these two would be given an additional payment of $1,500 a year. To cover this new expense, each member was assessed $500, to be paid to Clark by July 1811.[42]

Before the departure of the relief mission, the company held another meeting to correct yet another problem that had arisen. William Morrison, upon returning to St. Louis from the first expedition, had purchased some of the company furs before turning them over to Clark for storage. This resulted in a dispute with Lisa, who claimed that Morrison had not paid the full price for the furs. With this incident in mind, the articles of agreement were amended to make it mandatory for all partners to relinquish their furs to Clark immediately upon arrival in St. Louis.[43]

With the return of the relief party and the groups led by Henry and Lewis, the first venture of the Missouri Fur Company ended. On January 23, 1812, the members of the company assembled and decided that a completely new organization with more efficiency and capital was needed to succeed in the Northwest. The existing association, everyone agreed, should be allowed to expire on March 7. The partners appointed Lisa and Pierre Chouteau to dispose of the company's assets and to divide the returns in equal shares. The very next day, on January 24, the members signed a new body of articles which created a partnership structured along corporate lines, with a president and a three-man board of directors designated to run the enterprise. The new company would have a capital stock of not more than fifty thousand dollars, of which twenty-three thousand dollars would be sold as public shares at one thousand dollars each. An annual stockholders' meeting would declare dividends and suggest needed changes in organization, the latter being subject to approval by two-thirds of the stockholders. Clark, as president, was to be paid six hundred dollars a year to defray the costs of storage and to hire clerks. The board of directors consisted of Manuel Lisa, Pierre Menard, and Sylvestre Labbadie. According to the new articles, only one member of the board would need to ascend the river yearly, for which he would receive a salary of one thousand dollars a year. The organization would be in effect until the first Monday in December, 1818, with the stipulation that two-thirds of the stockholders could dissolve it at any time.[44]

The response to the public sale of shares in the Missouri Fur Company proved disappointing. Impending hostilities with Great Britain made such a speculative venture too great a risk for St. Louis merchants. In order to obtain enough capital to operate, the board of directors appealed to every stockholder to advance thirty-six hundred dollars in cash and five thousand dollars more in credit. This request met with an equally bad response. Clark and Lisa finally put up notes for ten thousand dollars to start the company on a sound financial base.[45] Despite the gloomy financial picture, the partners felt that Lisa, upon his arrival upstream, would be able to immediately send furs from the posts already established on his first venture.

In May, 1812, the reorganized Missouri Fur Company embarked on its second venture. This consisted of a small expedition carrying eleven thousand dollars worth of merchandise in two boats. The furs expected from Lisa failed to arrive before the first annual meeting, held in December, 1812, and the members were told that only nine thousand dollars worth of furs were being sent down the river. This amount, however, did not cover the cost of outfitting the expedition. Displaying their lack of confidence, the stockholders voted to remove Lisa from the board of directors and to replace him with Pierre Chouteau. When Lisa did return, however, his cargo of furs proved far more valuable than the members had anticipated. He brought with him ten thousand dollars worth of beaver skins and from twelve to fifteen thousand dollars worth of buffalo robes.[46]

The future still looked dismal for the Missouri Fur

Company because the impending hostility between Great Britain and the United States finally ended in a declaration of war on June 18, 1812. With the primary concern in St. Louis now turned to defense of the town, on September 10, 1813, a meeting was set to dissolve the Missouri Fur Company.[47]

Final dissolution of the company occurred on June 16, 1814, with the sale of company assets and settlement of its financial responsibilities.[48] The Missouri Fur Company failed largely due to the lack of fluid capital on the frontier and the partners unwillingness to speculate in the face of pending hostilities between the United States and Great Britain. Manuel Lisa and William Clark were the most persistent in continuing the venture. Both Clark and Lisa advanced ten thousand dollars to insure the stability of the reorganized venture.

Both men showed financial courage in this matter because they invested their money at a time when impending war with Great Britain and Indian hostilities scared off most potential investors. Clark's drive, however, cannot be considered in the same light as Lisa's. Lisa's concern for success was marked by visions of a fur-trade monopoly in the Northwest. Though he, too, hoped to achieve financial success, Clark envisioned the Missouri Fur Company as an essential agent supporting America's claim to the Northwest, a goal that would be mutually beneficial to private and national interests. The distinction between the attitudes of the two men can also be drawn in their conception of the Indian. Lisa saw the Indian as a necessary cog in the fur trade, while Clark envisioned him as a key figure in support of immediate national interests and as a viable, assimilated member of American society.[49]

Clark's conception of the role of the Indian and the territories in the national scheme was dealt a severe blow by the War of 1812 because this conflict served to accelerate intellectual change in the early nineteenth century, a change that inside of a decade made Jefferson's ambitious programs anachronistic. With the end of the War of 1812, the nation no longer feared for its security. It instead concentrated more on settling and exploiting the western territories than on securing them in a colonial scheme. Jefferson's fears of populating the West were no longer important amidst dreams of abundance. It was these dreams integrally mixed with the West that became part of the incomprehensibly bright future of the young nation, a future that promised riches for anyone who had the ambition to seek them out. The traditional values of Jefferson's age fell to the immediate wants of the individual. As the new age advanced, some members of the old order adjusted while others became increasingly alienated. William Clark's future was shaped largely in terms of such a struggle.

"The BLOOD of our citizens cryed aloud for VENGEANCE. The general cry is let the north as well as the south be JACKSONIZED!!!"[1]

The War of 1812 in the West

The United States officially declared war on Great Britain on June 18, 1812, but to Clark and citizens of the western territories the war had begun as early as 1811 when Indians amassed again, as in 1809, around the camp of the Prophet and his brother Tecumseh in the Indian territory near Tippecanoe Creek. William Henry Harrison, seeing a chance to destroy the menacing influence of the two great chiefs, attacked their village on November 16, 1811, destroying it and forcing the Indians to retreat. After this, individuals and communities throughout the West suffered Indian reprisals.

These developments must necessarily be seen from the perspective of the white settler, the Indian, and Jeffersonian Indian policy. The period of white-Indian relations in the Ohio and Mississippi valleys between the end of the initial Indian wars in 1795 and the outbreak of the War of 1812 was muddled by different conceptions of what was transpiring. From 1800, with the onset of Jeffersonian Indian policy, attempts were made to adjust the environmental conditions of the Indian in order to accelerate his assimilation into American life. From a Jeffersonian perspective it was assumed that, because of the mechanistic relationship between environment (agricultural plots) and man (the Indian), an Indian yeoman farmer would emerge with the same ambitions and desires as Western man. Thus during this period the territorial governors of Indiana and Michigan, William Henry Harrison and William Hull, coerced and negotiated treaty after treaty which ceded millions of acres of Indian lands to the United States.

From the perspective of the American Indian, on the other hand, this period was one of gradual awareness that the cession of land was becoming a never-ending process. It was felt that enough land cessions had been made to the American intruders and that it was now time to defend what land was remaining. The great Shawnee leader Tecumseh eloquently reflected these sentiments:

> *The white race is a wicked race. Since the day when the white race had first come in contact with the red men, there had been a continual series of aggressions. Their hunting grounds were fast disappearing, and they were driving the red men farther and farther to the west. Such had been the fate of the Shawnees, and surely that would be the fate of . . . [all tribes] if the power of the whites was not forever crushed. The mere presence of the white man was a source of evil to the red man. His whiskey was destroying the bravery of their warriors, and his lust corrupting the virtue of their women. The only hope for the red man was a war of extermination against the paleface.*[2]

The conceptual barrier that existed between Jeffersonian policy and the Indians' view regarding land acquisition gave Jefferson's policy little chance of success.

From the perspective of the white settler, the outbreak of the War of 1812 was but an escalation of the Indian depredations and hostilities they had faced for decades on the frontier. From their point of view, neither the inter-

national implications of the war nor the Jeffersonian program of Indian assimilation were of great interest. What
mattered most was that their chances of economic success
on the frontier were being jeopardized and, ultimately,
their lives endangered by the Indian while the federal
government appeared to be ignoring their interests.

By the time the War of 1812 had been officially declared, the territories were already mobilized for defense.
Benjamin Howard, the successor to Lewis as the governor
of the Missouri Territory, mustered regulars and newly
organized militia to patrol known trouble spots. He placed
special emphasis on the northern sector of the territory,
especially along the Mississippi River in the area of
Prairie du Chien. As a result, few military units were
available west of the Mississippi River. In the entire area
west of the Mississippi there were, on June 6, 1812, only
241 regular troops scattered at Fort Osage, Fort Madison,
and Fort Bellefontaine.[3]

With the defense of the frontier in such a pitiful state
and regular reports in the *Missouri Gazette* of Indians
massing in the Great Lakes region for an attack on St.
Louis, the area became a tense place in which to live
during the war years. Territorial citizens knew all too well
that the region around St. Louis blocked British access to
New Orleans. Kate L. Gregg perhaps captured the mood
of the West during the War of 1812 best when she wrote:
"False reports and flying rumors fell on ears ready to hear,
tongues ready to wag. Sickening truth, false alarms, and
general uncertainty all combined to create the frontier
psychology which is the outstanding feature of the War of
1812 in the West."[4]

On July 25, 1812, the *Missouri Gazette* reported the
presence of seventy Winnebago, Ioway, and Otto Indians
between Fort Osage and Boonslick, about one hundred

Sacs above Fort Madison, and five hundred Indians in Illinois waiting to attack. Two weeks later the *Gazette* reported twelved hundred Indians gathered at Peoria, Illinois, ready to attack American posts.[5] While rumors of large Indian gatherings most often proved false, there were enough skirmishes on the frontier to cause Governor Howard and Governor Ninian Edwards of Illinois to travel to Washington to seek increased federal assistance. Federal officials, however, considered the crucial theaters of the War of 1812 to be mainly in the East and in the Great Lakes region, perhaps no farther west than Detroit. The two territorial governors, consequently, received no direct assistance and managed only to obtain approval to arm ten more companies of rangers.[6]

While officials correctly stressed the war in the East, a very real war was being waged in the West. It began as an economic war to gain allegiance of the Indians, but it soon became a real war waged by British traders and their Indian allies. While federal officials did not consider the West crucial in their plans to win the war, they did have a program of defense for the frontier region. That program involved keeping the Indians neutral and safeguarding the frontier from the Ohio River to the Missouri River through a system of fortified posts and mounted patrols which the Congress had authorized governors Howard and Edwards to enlist. Finally, and a matter of most concern to William Clark, there were plans to construct a fort at Prairie du Chien to counter British access to the tribes trading at that post.[7] This fort became necessary after the fall of the Mackinac Island post on July 17, 1812, allowed the British to roam freely the upper Mississippi, trading and spreading ill will against the Americans. Because of demands of the war in the East, the fort was not constructed until Clark attempted it on his own in 1814.

The winter of 1812–13 proved an especially apprehensive time to territorial citizens because they learned that British agents and their Indian allies were gathering at Prairie du Chien. Expecting the worst, officials in St. Louis became convinced that a British fort would be constructed at Prairie du Chien as a base for a spring offensive against St. Louis. But spring saw the Prairie du Chien complement move north for action in Canada to counter American advances there, leaving the lower Missouri region free from full-scale attack but nevertheless plagued with small guerilla-type raids. Governor Howard, without further federal assistance, decided to consolidate his troops by closing Fort Osage and moving those at Fort Mason down the Mississippi to a point closer to St. Louis. By the fall of 1813, Fort Madison, which had been maintained earlier, was also finally abandoned.[8]

In the spring of 1813, Clark again visited Washington to confer with the new secretary of war, John Armstrong, about the Indian situation on the Mississippi and Missouri rivers. While he was there, President Madison appointed Clark governor of the Missouri Territory and consolidated Indian affairs with that office. Clark left Washington in April, and, upon arriving in St. Louis, he was given his official commission as governor, dated June 16, 1813.[9]

As governor, Clark took charge of frontier defenses and continued with his previous responsibilities concerning Indian diplomacy. Clark's energetic and efficient nature were immediately evident. He began from scratch by asking all of the Indian agents and factors to send him a thorough report on the quantity of assets in their possession, the number of Indians in their agency, and an evaluation of the latter's disposition towards the United States. He wanted also a list of citizens injured or killed by the tribes and the amount of property destroyed or taken by the Indians. From this information Clark hoped to separate fact from rumor and make his efforts against the British and their Indian allies more effective.[10]

He next moved the friendly Sac and Fox Indians from the northern frontier region to an area south of the Missouri River near the territory of the Osage Indians. He did not want these tribes to be influenced by the more belligerent Indians of the upper Mississippi, especially those of the Rock River region near Prairie du Chien. Clark appointed John Johnson, the factor of the recently abandoned Fort Madison, to establish a factory on the Little Moniteau Creek for the newly moved tribes. Clark also asked George Sibley to re-establish his factory for the Osages at Arrow Rock on the Missouri River.[11]

As an integral part of his program of defense Clark also had four armed barges built to patrol the Mississippi and Illinois rivers. Clark's crisis mentality led him to fund the project personally before seeking federal aid. Explaining his haste, he reasoned:

The preparing of these Gun boats is not by the directions of the Government; but impressed with the fullest assurence of the necessity of those points being guarded without delay, and as there was not sufficient time to get directions from the Government at so great a distance; [I] directed the Boats prepared for defence, and made the advances necessary to Complete them under an expectation of the measure being adopted.[12]

Fortunately for Clark, the measure was adopted, and he was eventually reimbursed.

Beyond approving funds for the armed barges, the federal government failed to give increased attention to the western theater of the war. In the winter of 1813 the federal government placed General Howard and his First Regiment under the command of the Eighteenth Regiment in Cincinnati for service in the eastern sector of the war. This left the militarily weak frontier almost defenseless. In an attempt to impress Washington officials with the plight of the West, Clark reported to the secretary of war that he had no regular troops remaining in the territory except for part of an artillery company. In addition, he had three companies of rangers and some volunteers to man the gunboats being built.[13]

By withdrawing regular troops, the federal government did not feel it was abandoning the western theater, for it believed the area to be secure in light of American victories in the Great Lakes region. Officials in St. Louis were not so certain. Clark received word that another force was gathering in Prairie du Chien, but he could not know that the troops involved there were regrouping for a spring defensive effort at Michilimackinac in the upper Great Lakes region. Clark, as well as the citizens of the territory, could only be sure that enemy forces were again massing in the North and that territorial forces were inadequate for defense.

Sentiment had been building in St. Louis for some type of offensive effort. Clark, too, had been toying with the idea of some sort of offensive thrust to the North. Earlier, when the government had advocated a fort at Prairie du Chien, he had wanted to push all the way to Green Bay to establish a defensive position. Such a maneuver, however, would have required considerable military strength. Unfortunately, in 1814, Clark did not have the military force or even the authority to take the offensive against Prairie du Chien.

The government order which transferred Howard to the Eighteenth Regiment in Cincinnati also transferred authority for the defense of the West out of the hands of the governors and into those of the Eighteenth Regiment.[14] Nevertheless, the tension that existed in St. Louis demanded some form of visible local action. Even Clark's wife may have exerted some pressure. She had a young family to think of: Meriwether Lewis, the first born, was only five years old, and William Preston only three, followed by the baby, Mary Margaret, who was not two months old. Julia wrote to her brother describing the happenings at Prairie du Chien and her own feeling of helplessness in that matter. She ended her letter with a fatalistic note, stating, "God only knows what our fate is to be. . . ."[15]

By the spring thaw of 1814, Clark had decided to act. Knowingly unequipped for anything as bold as occupying Prairie du Chien and establishing a fort, he planned instead to wage a harassing hit-and-run campaign by using the most effective military device he had left—the gunboats. As preparations for the campaign proceeded, Major Zachary Taylor unexpectedly arrived in St. Louis with a company of sixty-one regulars. The additional men gave Clark confidence to attempt a bolder maneuver by occupying the post at Prairie du Chien and constructing a fort there. On May 4, 1814, Clark informed the secretary of war of the expedition and its goals of manning the fort with sixty-one men, leaving two gunboats in the area for protection.[16]

Clark's plan proceeded with ease as the expedition occupied Prairie du Chien on June 2 without opposition. The main British body had left twenty days earlier, accompanied by three hundred Indians. The small force left to defend the site fled when Clark approached. Proceeding as planned, Major Taylor's men began building the fortifications under the guard of the two gunboats, while Clark returned to St. Louis fully confident of the permanence of his accomplishment. Clark felt so secure that he even recommended moving Johnson's factory to Prairie du Chien.[17]

Clark's optimism proved to be premature. On July 17, 1814, a force of twelve to fifteen hundred Indians laid siege to the newly christened Fort Shelby, and two days later, with the gunboats driven away, the Americans surrendered. The fall of Fort Shelby constituted the final blow to Clark's strategy, for in the interim even the lower Missouri tribes had revolted. The Sac and Fox tribes, and even the Osages, had shown signs of belligerency all spring, resulting in Sibley and Johnson abandoning their relocated factories and fleeing with their goods to St. Louis.[18]

The increase of Indian raids on the lower Missouri enraged the settlers, as indicated in the *Missouri Gazette* which, instead of reporting the usual fearful account of the war in the West, blurted: "The BLOOD of our citizens cryed aloud for VENGEANCE. The general cry is let the north as well as the south be JACKSONIZED!!!"[19] The blast referred to a more militant policy toward the Indian as ascribed to the well-known Indian fighter, Andrew Jackson. Christian Wilt, a St. Louis merchant, echoed the same sentiment when he wrote to an associate that he favored "slaying every Indian from here to the Rocky Mountains."[20] Even Clark came under criticism. People began to question whether an Indian agent could ever punish the Indians in the manner which they deserved.

This is yet another indication of the growing gap between Clark and the white settlers of the frontier. The settler could see only Indian atrocities and the necessity for reprisal. Clark, as a nationally appointed official, remained oriented to the ideals of the earlier Jeffersonian programs. He still stressed Indian diplomacy and assimilation in the context of securing the western territories for American national interests. The economic and diplomatic warfare that Clark had engaged in since coming to St. Louis in 1807 had now turned to actual battlefield combat, and it called for desperate measures.

Clark appointed a highly experienced man in Indian relations, Manuel Lisa, to go among the friendly tribes on the Missouri and persuade them to make war against the hostile Indians of the Mississippi.[21] With winter arriving in Missouri, another British miliatry buildup occurred in Prairie du Chien, and with it renewed fears of an all-out attack from the North gripped the citizens of Missouri.

The news of the peace at Ghent signed on December 24, 1814, did little to ease the fears of the beleaguered citizens of the Territory of Missouri. In fact, they felt it worsened their situation. The treaty, as applied to their situation, did not allow them to precipitate any military action against the Indians pending a treaty session with the latter which was scheduled for July of 1815. The session was six months away, and it was felt that the Indians could do a great deal of harm in the interim. Missouri officials spent the winter of 1814–15 seeking federal military assistance. Rufus Easton, the Missouri territorial delegate, was busy trying to convince Washington officials that the territories needed more military protection, at least until the peace conference in July.

In addition to the physical harm suffered by the region, the war caused serious economic problems. St. Louis, a bustling trade center before the war, almost shut down during the war years. Christian Wilt referred to the situation as early as 1812: "all kinds of business is stopped since the war. We sell nothing."[22] Clark sent representatives to Washington to obtain the back pay due rangers and militia who had served during the war.[23] Once that had been obtained, merchants could hope to receive payment for goods advanced by them to the militia in preceding months.

Clark spent the winter of 1814–15 making new preparations to handle the anticipated Indian problems in the spring. Missouri's congressional delegate, Rufus Easton, had no visible success in obtaining more military strength for the territory. In fact, as late as February 25, he had produced no additional troops for Missouri. Not relying on federal officials, Clark persuaded the Missouri territorial legislature to pass a conscription bill giving him the power to draft able-bodied men into the service.[24] As spring arrived, the anticipated "attrocities" began to occur regularly. The *Missouri Gazette* no longer mentioned such raids with the usual detachment of a military report. Its pages contained explicit details, such as the following account:

Mrs. Ramsey was attending the milking of her cows, and her pretty little children were amusing themselves feeding the poultry and assisting their mother. Mr. Ramsey, who you know has but one leg was near his wife at the moment the first shot was fired. He seen his wife fall and succeeded to lead her into the house, but as he reached the door he received a wound which prevented him to go to the relief of his children who were caught by the indians and cut to pieces in the yard. Mr. and Mrs. Ramsey are dead, both were shot through the abdomen.[25]

It was in this tense atmosphere that William Clark, Auguste Chouteau, and Governor Ninian Edwards were appointed commissioners to make peace with the warring Indians. Prospects for a peace conference got an ominous start when the gunboat sent by the commission to the Rock

River tribes to announce the site and time of the conference was driven back by hostile Indians without making
contact. The commission next sent two French trappers
who succeeded in making contact but brought back a
pessimistic report. The trappers indicated that the Indians
remained very much under British influence and had
every intention of continuing the war. The commissioners
suspected more and more that the only effective deterrent
would be a massive show of strength on the part of the
Americans.[26]

The commission nevertheless went ahead with its plans
and announced that a conference would be held on July 1,
1815, at Portage de Sioux on the Mississippi. It implored
the citizens of Missouri and Illinois to refrain from harm-
ing the tribes on their way to the conference. George
Sibley and John Johnson were assigned to obtain thirty
thousand dollars worth of presents to be given to the Indians. The news of the gifts enraged Missouri citizens who
were not in a forgiving mood. The *Missouri Gazette*, for
example, felt it would be far better to give the presents
to the widows and orphans of the murdered white settlers.[27]

On July 5, 1815, four days late, the conference began in
a well-organized manner. Clark, dressed in a black suit
with a high collar and white stock, gave the opening address at the council. There seems to have been an unwritten
understanding that Clark was the head of the commission,
for he was the first to address the council. His name also
appears first among the commissioners on the Indian
treaties, followed by Governor Edwards and Auguste
Chouteau. Clark opened the council by welcoming all of
the tribes, specifically relating his comments to their individual attitudes towards the Americans before and
after the war. Clark's references to the tribes individually
demonstrates that he did not conceive of them in a mono-

lithic sense and that he wanted them to feel a personal relationship to him and to the other commissioners representing the United States government. He closed his address by turning to a delegation of Rock River Sacs who had been particularly belligerent toward the council and expressed regret that their leaders were not present. He indicated that if they did not appear before him in thirty days, he would consider them at war.[28]

After addresses by Edwards and Chouteau, the commission met with each tribe individually to draw up peace treaties. Each pact was essentially the same, indicating a mutual forgiveness and recognition of a peaceful status between the two parties. In addition, both signatories agreed to release all prisoners held at the time. The ceremony was completed by giving the Indians presents to compensate for their dead. The entire conference lasted more than three months, with the final treaty being signed on September 16, 1815. After the commission returned to St. Louis, additional peace agreements were drawn up in October with the Kansas Indians and the following spring with the hostile Rock River Sacs.[29]

Even with the conclusion of the treaty-making process, the commissioners, and no doubt the citizens of the western territories, doubted that it would last. In a joint letter to the secretary of war the commissioners made known their fears. "A number of British traders, with goods to a great amount, on which they have paid no duties, have arrived on the Mississippi and we feel well assured that many of the difficulties that have occured [sic] with the Indian, and which will continue are justly attributable to that class of people."[30]

With a temporary lull in Indian hostilities, Clark resumed an attitude characteristic of the Jeffersonian policy that had preceded the War of 1812. Rather than emphasize the increasing role of the white settler, Clark returned to a colonial conception of the territory and the importance of the fur trader in securing it. Clark seemed more determined than ever to achieve some stability in the fur trade and thus prevent a recurrence of all the hostilities that had just terminated. In Clark's view the war had done nothing to change the ingredients that had produced the hostilities. Competitive British and American traders were still creating ill will among the Indians.

In a letter to the secretary of war on October 1, 1815, Clark specifically stated what he felt was needed to improve the fur-trade situation. First he advocated that Indian agents be given much more power to carry out existing laws. He felt that the agent was too restricted to be effective in detecting illicit trade or in settling disputes between Indians and whites. He also warned against forming an overly rigid system for dealing with the Indian because he felt they differed "materially in disposition, habits, manners, customs, and trade. . . ."[31] Clark further suggested that agents for the Indian trade and the diplomatic Indian agents be consolidated in one department, "considering that trade is the great lever by which to direct the policy and conduct of the Indian tribes toward the United States."[32] In other words, Clark saw no distinction between the commercial and political relationships of the Indian to the United States. These were all integrated in one national design—consolidating and securing the empire.

Further evidence of Jeffersonian concepts is seen in Clark's qualified endorsement of the factory system, at a time when there were increasing pressures from private trading interests and a general aura of suspicion over government interference in local economic matters. Clark indicated that a well-placed and well-managed factory could be "extremely useful and instead of being expensive, (I am told), are profitable to the Government."[33] He qualified his endorsement of the factory by indicating that it would function best in a well-settled area where proper supervision could be given the trade. Currently the trade was too scattered for the factory to achieve maximum effectiveness.

Because conditions were not suitable for the optimum use of the factory system, Clark provided his own suggestion for an effective trade policy. He felt that it should consist of a

> . . . well organized company with a large capital and a liberal aid and protection from the Government. . . . it must be a company sufficiently powerful to take in hand all the trade of the Missouri and Upper Mississippi . . . in cooperation with, and partly under the direction of the Government. Its capital ought to be large (say 600,000 or 1,000,000 dollars), divided in small shares (say 100 dollars each share, to enable the most indigent trader to become interested). . . .[34]

Clark suggested that a company of the size he proposed would have a monopoly on the fur trade. A monopoly, in Jeffersonian terms, did not contain all of the negative aspects that can be associated with the term since that time. On the contrary, a monopoly from Clark's view meant the elimination of the harmful competitive practices that led traders too often to cheat and deceive the Indian, thus placing the government in a bad light. In the Jeffersonian sense a monopoly had to consider the societal welfare as well. Therefore, Clark proposed that the shares be small enough to include even "the most indigent trader." Of course it was assumed that Clark's giant company would be carefully regulated by the government, much as the British government controlled its fur companies. As late as 1831, Clark suggested that Americans adopt British methods in the fur trade. He referred to such methods as "rather despotic, yet Salutary. . . ." and went on to state, "Instances are within the recollection of persons yet living of the most rigorous measures pursued by the British Government against improper conduct toward, the Indians; and whose wealth and Standing could not prevent their Exclusion forever after from the Indian Country. . . ."[35]

In another communiqué Clark outlined how the entire societal structure would benefit by such an organization:

A company thus powerful would be able to furnish all the indian tribes with the best of goods, and would, without doubt, sweep the whole of the valuable fur trade of the Missouri and Mississippi; expel all the petty (though now very powerful) British traders; and bring into our markets immense quantities of the most valuable furs and peltries. . . .

An establishment of this sort would interest a vast number of our Western citizens in the well-managing of our Indian affairs; it would attract the attention of enterprising Americans, and give employment to the most of our citizens who are accustomed to trade with the Indians, and be the means of discovering and drawing forth for the use and comfort of our own country.

It would effectively draw out and keep out that restless and deadly hostile influence that has been heretofore used so successfully among the Indians to our prejudice by the British traders and agents. . . .

A company such as I have been speaking of would be a combination of American capital and American traders to draw out foreign traders who are intruding without permission, and to place the Indian relations more under the control and management of the Government. . . .[36]

Such was Clark's frame of reference for the Missouri Territory as well as for the Indian trade in the western territories. He clearly demonstrated that he still conceived of the western territories in a colonial scheme. The end of the War of 1812 was, however, a changing point in Clark's career. To that time he was in the vanguard of his nation's development, since the western territories were still conceived of as colonies. After the war's conclusion and resulting changes, Clark's worldview went against the current of American development. He stressed trade at a time when the territory he governed was becoming increasingly dominated by white agricultural settlers. He stressed government monopolies in an age that was clamoring more and more for private free enterprise. The conceptual gap that separated William Clark, as implementor of Jeffersonian ideals, and the white settler eventually crystallized into an ideological gap, one which is clearly revealed in Clark's association with Missouri territorial politics from 1813 to 1820.

VII

Clark Versus the New Order

The creation of the Missouri Territory in 1813 came in the middle of an era of extraordinary change in American political thought. In these early decades of the nineteenth century, the erosion of Jeffersonian political values was completed, culminating in 1828 with the election of Andrew Jackson. Throughout its territorial days, Missouri was deeply involved in the fur trade, and its political affairs were dominated by fur-trading interests. After the War of 1812, however, agrarian elements began to make their influence felt because of the increasing numbers of farmers coming to the region in search of homes.

As the farming frontier gradually replaced the fur-trading frontier, societal and cultural values changed. A partial explanation for intellectual change in early nineteenth-century Missouri lies in the distinctions between these two frontiers. The fur-trading frontier might be thought of as an expeditionary frontier, while the farming frontier was sedentary. The importance of this distinction is that on an expeditionary frontier there seems to have been an absence of a "settling" mentality. Instead, there was a sense of being only temporarily removed from civilization. The effect seems to have been one of an individual retaining the value structure which he brought

105

with him. On the farming frontier there was an equal sense of being removed from civilization, but with one important distinction—the settler had no intention of returning. Thus individuals on the farming frontier became involved in building their own civilization, and, in the process of attempting to recreate established values, expediency to meet environmental circumstances seems to have unconsciously eroded some of the manners and customs originally brought to the frontier. Out of these circumstances arose the early sentiments that eventually matured into a mentality attributed to a Jacksonian intellectual framework. The earlier economic order, which saw the interrelationship of individual and national interests, was completely inverted. The new order stressed individual interests and the freedom of individuals to pursue their interests unencumbered by regulation as the best method of realizing national prosperity.[2]

Along with this came a whole new sense concerning the role of politics and leadership and the citizens' relation to government. With the new stress on individual interests, it naturally followed that citizens no longer thought so much in terms of choosing judicious leadership as they did of choosing leaders who would represent their own local and personal interests. Indeed, the slow and subtle erosion of values which had permeated the frontier regions since colonial times seems to have crystallized into a conscious American thought and creed during the early nineteenth century. Nowhere can the dynamics of this change be more clearly seen than in Missouri territorial politics from 1813 to 1820.

Owing to the relative security produced by the end of the War of 1812, a new wave of immigration flooded the territory. Missouri's population grew from twenty-five thousand in 1814 to over sixty-six thousand in 1820. Missouri had much to attract new settlers with its continuing fur trade and developing lead-mining industry. Even more important to Missouri's rapid growth during these years was the clamor for new farming lands on the part of the settlers.

In response to the great demand for land, prices soared as speculators eagerly greeted new arrivals to the territory. The *Missouri Gazette* contained many printed notices of new land offices being opened. The land boom in Missouri, however, had in it the ingredients that produced friction in Missouri politics. Because of the haphazard manner in which the Spanish had granted tracts of land, it now became necessary for American officials, after the Louisiana Purchase, to distinguish between legitimate and fraudulent claims. In 1805 the United States government established a board of commissioners to decide the fate of disputed land claims. Although the government followed a liberal policy in validating Spanish land claims, when the commission completed its work in 1812, the land question was only beginning to generate discord.

An earthquake in the New Madrid district of the Missouri Territory in 1811 caused more confusion in the land situation. Many settlers who were left homeless by that disaster received relief from the government in the form of land certificates to relocate, usually in the Boonslick region, free of cost.[3] The situation was ripe for deception, because speculators purchased the New Madrid certificates, sometimes before the quake victims were aware of the government's relief efforts. Many New Madrid claimants who did relocate on better land often found that the tracts they had hoped to settle were already claimed under a Spanish land grant. This situation produced yet another ingredient in the land problem—the squatter.

Because of the desire for new land, speculators and settlers urged the federal government to make additional lands available to the public. Although reluctant to do so because some of the less desirable lands already opened to settlement still remained unoccupied, the federal government finally announced that additional public lands would be offered for sale in August of 1818.[4] Some eager settlers did not wait for the sale but simply squatted on government and Indian lands under the assumption that at a future date, when the region would be put up for sale, they would have pre-emption rights to acquire their holdings. However, pre-emptive rights were not forthcoming until 1819, and in the interim many squatters lost confidence and bought New Madrid certificates at inflated prices.[5]

The land situation and the havoc it produced also contributed to a new consciousness of local interests and to their political expression through interest-group politics, which manifested itself in Missouri as political factionalism. Factions rather than parties characterized the period because most Missourians professed some shade of Republicanism, thereby concentrating rivalries on local issues and personalities. Two groups emerged. One group, labeled the "little junto" by Joseph Charless, editor of the *Missouri Gazette*, consisted basically of the established French families and older government employees, most of whom owned large tracts of land under the Spanish land-grant system. This group had the support of the fur-trading interests led by Auguste Chouteau and was politically represented by William Clark, John Scott, and Thomas Hart Benton. The other group, largely made up of individuals who had come to Missouri after the Louisiana Purchase, consisted of young lawyers and land speculators, such as Joseph Charless, the territorial delegate Rufus Easton, and a member of the board of the land commissioners, J. B. C. Lucas, and his son, Charles.[6]

As the political standard-bearer of the little junto, Clark has been swept into the mainstream of Missouri politics by students of that subject who have depicted the political situation as one of opposing interest groups battling for control of the territory.[7] While this may be an accurate assumption to use in studying territorial politics, it does not account for how Clark, for example, related to that faction or how he conceived of his role as governor of the territory. Equally important, it is necessary to go beyond the above description of circumstances that affected the Missouri political climate to understand how Missourians conceived of these developments and how they conceived of Clark as their political leader. If this is done, two images of Clark emerge—his own and that of the citizens of Missouri.

Missourians related to Clark not through Clark's conceptions of the territory, but on the more overt level of his association with the little junto and his implementation of federal programs, both of which were seen as contributors to the citizens' problems. Aside from his being the implementer of federal programs, the Missourians' image of Clark as a political figure could not be disentangled from that of the self-interests of the little junto. Clark's own image of his association with the little junto was, however, of an entirely different nature. His political actions from 1815 to 1820 demonstrate that he continued to identify with the territory in terms of national goals. For this reason he understandably identified with the little junto. Its fur trade and commercial interests were more closely attuned to the broader colonial scheme that Clark brought to the territory. In 1817, as an indication of the conceptual gap that existed between Clark and the prevailing sentiment in the territory, local-interest advocates in St. Louis were toasting each other on the Fourth of July in the following manner:

The Lead & Fur Trade of the country—Certain sources of wealth and strength if in the hands of individuals. But not otherwise. . . .
Salt Springs & Public Lands in the territory—May they be speedily offered for sale; better in the government.[8]

Clark, on the other hand, in writing to Thomas Jefferson less than a year earlier, demonstrated a much broader concern for the territory:

. . . the upper and richer portion [Missouri River] has had no American Citizen since the falur of the Missouri C. [Missouri Fur Company of] 1811 and I am under great apprehentions that the British will take possessions of that rich Tract. . . . If a large and overbearing company cannot be formed of American citizens with sufficient capital to keep them out. . . .[9]

Clark's broader view of the territory also caused him to identify much more closely with individual members of the little junto, such as Auguste Chouteau. This seems significant, for while Chouteau was perhaps the most powerful and aggressive businessman in the territory, he demonstrated the promotion of his own interests through a broader vision of the territory. This can be seen not only in the far-reaching arena of Chouteau's economic concerns, the fur trade, but also in his willingness to serve on governmental commissions.

It must be emphasized at this point that although men like Chouteau and Clark possessed more traditional notions of the economic order, they were no less concerned with their own interests than any other generation of men. But unlike their Jacksonian counterpart, they saw their own best interests as indistinguishably tied to a larger societal or national unit. In other words, in order for them to prosper, the nation-state must first prosper. The Jacksonian man seems to have had an inverted sense of economic order. From his perspective he felt that he must be left alone to prosper in order for the nation-state to prosper. Likewise, the new settler no longer conceived of the interests of the territory as indistinguishably bound up with the interests of the nation as a whole, as did Clark.

Unlike his image in the eyes of Missouri settlers, Clark differed with other members of the little junto on some issues. Clark, for example, had fewer personal economic interests at stake in the political struggle between the factions and therefore on some issues actually opposed his faction. Thus in the disputed land situation, for example, Clark expressed his sympathy not for the Spanish land claimant but for the squatters, especially for those who defended the area during the War of 1812.[10] In addition, while his political colleagues sought to discontinue the government's Indian factory system, Clark defended it. Such, then, was the complex interplay of forces and associations that set the stage for political confrontation in Missouri politics in the popular elections of 1816, 1817, and 1820.

The election of a territorial delegate in 1816 represented the first significant confrontation of opposing forces in Missouri territorial politics. The territorial delegate had no vote in Congress, yet he was the closest link between the territory and national officials, causing the contest to be bitterly fought.

The little junto candidate, John Scott, an attorney from Ste. Genevieve, challenged the incumbent territorial delegate, Rufus Easton. Scott opened his campaign in the winter of 1815 on a platform similar to Easton's which pledged to end government monopoly of mineral lands, to dismantle the government factory system, to work for the quick admission of Missouri to statehood, to oppose removal of squatters, and to work for internal improvements.[11] The demands of Missourians were clear, and it was political suicide to counter them.

Because both factions espoused the same platform, attention necessarily had to be directed at the candidates personally. Scott's supporters pointed to Easton's involvements in land specualtion and to his large holdings as explanations for his efforts to get more public land put up for sale. In addition, they attributed Easton's efforts to block Spanish land claims as due to protection of his own land holdings. Easton's supporters, on the other hand, referred to Scott as part of a faction of lawyers and government officials in Missouri who sought to dominate the territory against the best interests of the public. And they also pointed to Scott's large holdings of Spanish land grants.[12]

Through association, Clark seemed very much a part of this political maneuvering in the eyes of the Missouri voters, but there is no evidence to contradict the notion that his role in Missouri politics was anything other than aimed at securing the nation's interests in territorial developments. This is especially significant because so much of his time was occupied during the War of 1812 with defending the territory against the British and their warring Indian allies and with securing peace treaties with the Indians in the years immediately following the war.[13]

During Clark's preoccupation with Indian matters, the Scott-Easton factions wound up their campaigns and awaited the results of their efforts on election day. Unfortunately for Clark, certain happenings on election day and his own premature declaration of Scott as the winner on September 16, 1816, caused a furor that reinforced the already questionable image of Clark in the minds of many Missouri voters.[14] Events are uncertain, but reportedly Scott was behind in the balloting, with all the votes in except those from the village of Cote Sans Dessein in the District of St. Charles. Supposedly, Scott himself rode to Cote Sans Dessein to obtain the remaining uncounted votes, whereupon Clark declared him the victor by fifteen votes without an official count.[15] Although Scott was known to be popular in the village, a bitter battle was set off that carried the disputed election all the way to Washington, where it was finally voided by Congress and a new election set for 1817.

The newspapers carried differing versions of the election with some interested parties reaffirming and others denying its validity. More important for the student of Clark's career are the severe attacks made against him for his part in the election, as these provide a focus on the political and intellectual mood of Missourians at the time. A letter to the *Missouri Gazette* signed by "Timoleon" effectively captured the mood of a beleaguered citizenry finally finding the courage to expose the autocratic Clark:

... *you seem to think that magical veil which has so long shrouded your public character with a borrowed sanctity, and has caused many to retire (they knew not why) at the very moment [they] was raised to assail you.... There is not a man of any standing in this country who has not, at some time or other been attacked for actions of a nature far less censerable than many of your official acts which have heretofore passed, and truth can no longer be smothered by official juggling and cabinet intrigue.*[16]

From that time on every public act of Clark's seemed to come under scrutiny. On January 31, 1817, Clark was criticized for signing a bill which established the Bank of Missouri. A letter written to the paper by "Cato" saw fit to relate the bank issue to larger matters concerning the principles of democratic government:

With the affrontery of a Cataline you have wontonly violated the principles of the American Government—you have prostrated the constitution and the laws of your country; and sported with the sacred rights of the people. These sir are serious, they are heavy charges and unfortunately for your political career, they are substantially true, and all have there origins in one single act of yours (aside from others) when you signed the paper you wish to be called the charter of the Bank of Missouri. . . .[17]

It is noteworthy that Cato was chosen as a pen name because as a Roman statesman (95–46 B.C.) he decried the declining morality of his time. The rhetoric of "Cato's" attack is equally noteworthy, for, like others still to be made on Clark, it did not confine itself rigidly to the issue at hand but dealt instead in generalities, indicating possibly that the Missourian had only a vague notion of the nature of the problems confronting him. In reality the bank bill went through the normal legislative process of receiving a majority vote in both territorial houses before being signed by Clark. Yet Clark alone was attacked for its passage.[18]

It seems clear that Clark served as a symbol for the general frustrations faced by the early nineteenth-century citizen of Missouri. This is not an unusual phenomenon. Historically, during periods of rapid change, institutions do not adequately cope with that change, and people, rather than recognize the inadequacy of their institutions, look for over-simplified explanations for their problems, usually symbolized in terms of an individual or a group. From 1815 to 1820, William Clark provided such a symbol. While the Missouri voter properly saw that the little junto might be dangerous to his own interests, he was wrong in blurring the distinction between Clark's motives for his own individual actions and the motives of the little junto. Therein lay the disparity between Clark's actions as expressed in the image of him held by Missourians and Clark's own conception of his actions.

The Missouri Territory lacked sufficient capital from its creation. In 1813 the Bank of St. Louis was chartered to serve this need; however, because of the delay in its organization, several businessmen backed out of the venture and applied for a charter for a new bank to be called the Bank of Missouri. The Bank of Missouri had a larger authorized operating capital, $250,000, as compared to the $150,000 of its predecessor, and it also had greater safeguards for the public. Still more important, while the first bank had been backed by local business interests with local concerns in mind, the Bank of Missouri had the support of the fur-trading merchants who, while perhaps concerned with their own economic interests, served the broader implications of national interests because of their roles as traders.[19]

Hence it is consistent that the new bank would foster the fur trade, which in Clark's view was indistinguishable from the interests of the western territories and American interests in the Northwest. The bank would, in short, help to check British influence in the American territory. Missourians, on the other hand, were less concerned with the Northwest than with Missouri and their own affairs, thereby failing to appreciate the underlying motives behind

Clark's actions. Easton supporters, however, well understood Clark's image in the minds of Missouri voters and
chose to capitalize on it in the upcoming election. Correspondence between two supporters of Easton indicated a
great deal of optimism about recent happenings and the
prospects of their candidate. "The Missouri Bank and
Gover. Clark's exertions in its support—and the close
political connection that exists between Clark-Scott-Hemp-
stead has done much towards reducing that party. . . .
Gov. C. is as unpopular as possible for a man to be."[20]

The next opportunity to censure Clark came after the
territorial legislature authorized the appointment of a
board of trustees to supervise the schools in St. Louis. In
1812, Congress passed an act that provided for public education in what was then Louisiana Territory. The act
provided that all town and village lots and all outlying
unclaimed lands not desired by the United States government were to be reserved for the support of public education. The appointment of a board of trustees in St. Louis
was one of the few efforts to activate the public education
act before statehood.[21] William Clark received appointment as chairman of the board by the territorial legislature,
the other members being Thomas Hart Benton, Auguste
Chouteau, Alexander McNair, Jean P. Cabanné, and William C. Carr.[22] Shortly thereafter, Clark, as chairman, ran
a notice in the *Missouri Gazette* that the bank was ready to
rent to the highest bidder houses, tenements, and lands
belonging by law to the schools. The notice went on to
state that "all persons who may be in possession of any
part of said property will immediately make known . . .
the nature and extent of their possessions, and from what
authority derived."[23] A week later a blast at the board, and
particularly Clark, appeared in the *Gazette*. Without men-
tioning any specific act of the board, it merely attacked the

manner in which the board came into existence, stating that a free people should have the right to elect such officials.[24] Here again is an example of how Clark, as the executive head and the symbol against self-rule, received the brunt of an attack not on a specific issue, but by general references to democratic procedures so jealously guarded by those of the new mentality.

On July 5, 1817, Clark announced that the first Monday in August would be set aside for a special election specified by Congress to elect a territorial delegate.[25] Here again some felt that Clark abused democratic procedures by not giving sufficient time for campaigning. On July 26, 1817, an anonymous letter to the *Gazette* castigated Clark for allowing so short a period for candidates to explain their virtues:

Every friend to the prosperity of the country, must be anxiously looking forward to the time, when we shall be enabled to emerge from our present degraded state. . . .

When, by the free voice of a free people, an honorable and independent man shall be selected from amongst us, to preside over, and direct the affairs of a great state. . . .

When we could say our governor always issues his proclamations time enough to reach the remote counties of Arkansas, before the day of election, and compell [sic] the people there to hold an election on the first monday of August, right or wrong. . . .[26]

It is true that Clark gave only a month's notice of the election date, an unduly short period of time under ordinary circumstances. It must also be remembered, however, that the candidates had already been campaigning for a year before the first election of 1816, and the voters by then well knew their platforms.

The same issue of the *Gazette* contained a letter inti-mating that Clark had arbitrarily dismissed some county officials without giving any reason to the people of Mis-souri. The general tone of the criticism implied that well-qualified people had been dismissed to make way for Clark cronies.[27] The letter referred to a Sergeant Hall who had been hired by Thomas Hart Benton as editor of the *St. Louis Enquirer*, a newspaper established to counter the anti-little junto *Missouri Gazette*. Frederick Billon, who had arrived in the territory in 1818, later recorded his impressions of the attempt to found another newspaper at about this time, 1814, as "certain prominent gentlemen of aristocratic tendencies, who from their lineage, posi-tion, and early training, had become leaders of society, and imagined themselves of bluer blood than the common herd. . . ."[28]

Events on election day served to further damage Clark's image in the eyes of the citizens of Missouri and to indicate to them that he was oblivious to their needs and desires. Upon emerging from the polling place on election day, Clark reportedly claimed in a loud voice that he had voted for John Scott.[29] While an honorable Republican practice in his native Virginia in the eighteenth century, this pub-lic declaration served to arouse public antipathy in nine-teenth-century Missouri.

To make matters worse, an unfortunate incident oc-curred on election day involving Clark's nephew, John O'Fallon, and Easton's brother-in-law, Dr. Robert Simp-son. O'Fallon, thinking he knew Simpson to be the author of several articles attacking Clark in the *Gazette*, pursued him at the polling center and shoved him with his elbow, whereupon Simpson drew a pistol. O'Fallon verbally in-sulted Simpson, causing Simpson to issue a challenge that he be given an opportunity to redeem his honor. Not having heard from Simpson, O'Fallon confronted him days later on the streets of St. Louis, calling him a liar and a coward. Again Simpson pulled a pistol, which O'Fallon wrestled from him. O'Fallon then proceeded to trounce his enemy.[30] This most unfortunate incident was associated with charges by the *Missouri Gazette* that infantrymen were roaming the streets of St. Louis on election day, intimidating Easton supporters with daggers, pistols, and clubs.[31] The *Gazette* went on to describe what it felt to be unsavory campaign techniques employed by Clark and the militia on election eve:

> *On Monday last, an election for delegate to congress took place in the several election districts of this territory. In this town, the election was conducted in the most violent, turbulent and savage manner.*
>
> *The night preceding the election the soldiers and music of a recruiting party, paraded the streets in the vicinity of the election ground, and early on Monday, the soldiers with labels or tickets on their caps, on which was printed "JOHN SCOTT" etc. were in possession of the ground with two stands of UNITED STATES COLORS on which "TRUE REPUBLICAN NOMINATION, John Scott," was printed or painted—a large shed, covered with boat sails was erected by some of the governor's family and others, near the door of the election, under which was spread tables covered with whiskey. . . .*[32]

A court of inquiry held to investigate the charges against the militia on election eve found them to be false and so dismissed the affair.[33] On September 27, 1817, after an official count, Clark announced that John Scott had won the special election with 2,406 votes to Easton's 2,014.[34]

Despite the opposition Clark was receiving in Missouri,

he was still regarded as a dependable public servant by the federal government. On June 21, 1817, he was reappointed governor of the Missouri Territory for his third term and reappointed again on February 10, 1820.[35]

During this period Clark found little release in his family life from the pressure of public duties. Julia, who had given birth to their fourth child, George Rogers Hancock Clark, on May 6, 1816, was in rapidly failing health in the spring of 1818 while carrying their fifth child. After the birth of John Julius on July 6, Julia's condition worsened.

With several years of severe public criticism behind him and his wife ailing, Clark decided temporarily to seek the more friendly confines of friends and relatives in Kentucky and Virginia. His absence brought only more criticism. Before his departure he had called the Missouri General Assembly into session, thus giving the appearance of indifference toward territorial affairs by leaving at such a time.[36] Thomas Forsyth wrote to Clark that winter in Louisville telling him of the mood of the legislature:

I have been told that some of the Legislative body have been grumbling about your not being here. . . . It is said by some people in this place that you make yourself very easy about this Ter'ty and the People in it as you are working to be appointed as Superintendent of Indian affairs as soon as we go into a State Government. . . .[37]

Leaving Julia behind, Clark returned to St. Louis briefly in the spring of 1819 to deal with some matters concerning his Indian agency before once again departing for Louisville in May. Later that year he and Julia made their way to Washington to visit President Monroe before traveling to Virginia to winter with her relatives.[38] Julia's health

Julia Hancock Clark, from a copy by Erganian of the Jarvis
portrait, Collection of Mrs. Daniel R. Russell (From *Persimmon
Hill: A Narative of Old St. Louis and the Far West*, by William
Clark Kennerly)

deteriorated to the point that doctors held little hope for her recovery. Clark himself was said to have been able to effect a recovery for his wife by blowing tar fumes into her lungs. In any event, her condition improved so that she was able to return to St. Louis with her husband in the spring of 1820. Meanwhile, events were occurring that would lead to the final conflict between the two battling factions in Missouri and to the end of William Clark's political career.

In March of 1820, Congress had passed an enabling act authorizing Missouri to write a constitution and form a state government. In May an election was held in which the fifteen counties chose delegates to attend the constitutional convention on June 12, 1820.[39] Clark's wife again took ill, causing him to leave the territory before the convention had completed its work. He therefore had little actual association with the constitution, but it did reflect his principles when it was completed.

The constitutional convention consisted of forty-one members split into three groups—liberal, conservative, and moderate. The liberal group of fourteen members favored frequent elections, no property qualification for voting, eligibility of naturalized citizens for the office of governor, prohibiting the lieutenant governor from voting in the legislature, and the popular election of local sheriffs and coroners. The general tenor of the liberal proposals lay in the direction of limiting the power of the executive and giving the people more control over the officials who governed them. Here again one can see the erosion of an earlier eighteenth-century notion which saw the need for screening leaders from the public so that they might rule judiciously, free from the pressures of specific interest groups or the whims of the masses.[40]

Opposing the liberal group on almost every principle

was a conservative faction of about sixteen delegates generally composed of the little junto faction and referred to in the convention as "the caucus." The third faction of about ten delegates split with the conservatives on some issues and thus constituted a mediating influence between the conservatives and the liberals.[41]

On July 19, 1820, the convention completed its work after five weeks of deliberation. The fourth Monday of August was set as the date for election of state officials.[42] On the whole, the completed constitution contradicted the prevailing mood of most Missourians. Because the liberal element represented this prevailing mood, it managed to incorporate some features such as universal manhood suffrage in the constitution, but it suffered defeat on most other issues. The liberal group failed in its efforts to restrict the power of the executive branch, to obtain restrictive banking regulations, and to shorten the term of representatives from two years to one. It failed to qualify naturalized citizens for the office of governor and to make the offices of sheriff and coroner elective.[43] Perhaps most obnoxious to the people of Missouri were the provisions in the constitution that forbade reduction of the salaries of the governor and judges during their tenure of office and gave all judicial officers lifetime appointments.[44] These provisions were offensive because they removed the executive and judicial branches from the immediate influence of the people.

In the opinion of many Missourians, the constitution had been written by those who had been dominating the territory since its beginning and who now expected to control the new state government. Many felt that a small caucus had dominated the convention and had already handpicked the men whom it wanted as state officials. Given such a mood on the part of the people, the liberals may have lost the battle in the convention, but they had ample ammunition for the upcoming state election.[45]

The convention spawned several candidates for the office of governor. Alexander McNair emerged as the leader of the liberal faction, gaining status by his efforts to change the constitution in favor of a more liberal amendment procedure.[46] In addition, Frederick Bates announced as a candidate with the backing of the St. Louis junto. With the announcement by the *Missouri Gazette* that William Clark was going to run for governor, however, Bates withdrew, and the caucus concentrated its support on Clark.[47]

Clark had not yet returned to the territory and would not do so until after the election. His wife, Julia, finally succumbed to her illness and died on June 27, 1820, in her native Virginia.[48] Clark made almost no personal effort to campaign for the office of governor, sending only two letters to the friendly *St. Louis Enquirer* less than a month before the election apologizing for being absent from the territory. In the second letter he wrote:

Fellow Citizens:

My name is before you as a candidate for the office of Governor of the new state of Missouri. A necessary absence, the cause of which is known to you, and I trust will be appreciated by you, will prevent me from being among you til the election is over. But this circumstance does not give me uneasiness, except as it may be construed by some into an indifference for your good will. Otherwise I think it of no importance for me to be present. The choice of the Governor is your business and not mine; and so far as my fitness for that place may be the subject of enquiry, that matter may be discussed as well in my absence as in my presence. I should take no part in the discussion even if I remained at home. . . .[49]

In this same letter to the *St. Louis Enquirer*, Clark demonstrated again his unawareness of the changing mood in
Missouri by referring to perhaps the most hated element
in the territory, the St. Louis Junto, as a reference for his
candidacy. He stated, "My long residence has given me a
personal acquaintance which time has ripened into friendship, with most of the old inhabitants and early settlers;
and to them I refer for answers to any inquiries which may
concern my individual and private character."[50] In addition, this correspondence contained the only effort on
Clark's part to state his own qualifications. In doing so he
made no reference to the themes so much in the minds of
Missourians at the time but emphasized instead his efforts
during the War of 1812 to keep the territory safe.[51]

Rather than cater to the specific interests of Missourians,
Clark seemed to emphasize a broader view of the position
of governor. As an appointed official he envisioned his
duties as that of a protector of the region in a military
sense and as an administrator of its affairs in line with
national interests. From Clark's perspective, local interests
were served best through the realization of national goals.

Clark and McNair both came from the upper stratum of
Missouri society. McNair was a large landowner, a military
officer, a businessman, and the register of the St. Louis
Land Office. The two men were close friends and remained so after McNair won the gubernatorial election.
In 1824, after McNair's term of office expired, Clark sought
to have him appointed as an Indian agent. Although the
two had similar backgrounds, McNair had canvassed the
territory during the election campaign and had displayed
a warm personality. He had apologized on occasion for
his lack of experience and had pledged to make the government more responsive to the people. He had criticized
the constitution and the men who wrote it, although he
never personally attacked Clark.[52] The same cannot be

said, however, for the backers of the two contestants. They waged a vicious campaign, especially in the press.

Perhaps the best insight into the mood of Missourians toward Clark can be seen in the rhetorical battles that took place in the neutral *Missouri Intelligencer* in Franklin. Articles appearing in that paper signed by an "Observer" set the tone of the campaign rhetoric by attacking McNair's ability to lead, stating that he could not even read.[53] A "Citizen" answered an earlier attack on McNair in strong language, declaring that "this 'Observer,' I know him, is such a captious, arrogant, dogmatic character . . . he assumes to himself a censorship over public opinion; . . . he fancies himself beyond control or check. . . . He imagines that his gigantic mind is the criterion of truth and correctness."[54] The "Observer," however, persisted in degrading McNair. "I admit him to be kind and charitable but his mind is not susceptible to cultivation."[55]

The "Observer" and the "Citizen" held entirely different conceptions of leadership. The "Observer" had natural aristocratic notions of leadership as opposed to the man-of-the-people view held by the "Citizen." The irony of this is that the little junto, representing an earlier form of republicanism, used the same rhetoric in the nineteenth century to defend itself as the Federalists had employed against the Republicans in the eighteenth century—referring to public spirit, aristocratic background, character, and perception.[56] The "democratic" element, on the other hand, represented in the nineteenth century what the Republicans had symbolized in the eighteenth century, namely a democratic government more responsive to the wishes of the people.

During the months preceding the election, the *Missouri Gazette* maintained a constant barrage of attacks on Clark. In issue after issue the *Gazette* methodically attempted to

point out Clark's weaknesses. It censured him for his
friendliness to the Indian at the expense of the white man,
for his frequent absences from the territory, and, of course,
for his arbitrary manner of handling the elections of the
territorial delegate in 1816 and 1817.[57] The final issue
before election day directly criticized Clark's personality
as being too "reserved, dignified, and unapproachable."[58]

As the election approached, Clark's supporters began to
lose hope that he might win. Clark's nephew, John O'Fallon, wrote to Dennis Fitzhugh, summing up Clark's chances.
"I had an opportunity of learning the sentiments of many
people with respect to the approaching election, the effect of which was confirming of my apprehensions that
Uncle Wm. will not be elected—his opponent will have a
hansome majority—[.] They accuse Governor Clark of
being friendly to the Indians, being stiff and reserved and
unhospitable."[59] O'Fallon was correct. The electorate gave
McNair 6,576 votes to Clark's 2,656.[60]

Thomas Hart Benton tried to explain Clark's defeat on
the grounds that his friends had deserted him under the
pressure of favorable reports about McNair's chances,
commenting that "the reports poured in from every quarter that he had no chance certainly contributed to the result. Many of his friends gave way under it."[61] Clark's
resounding defeat, however, paralleled that of other convention delegates associated with the caucus who ran for
offices under the new state government. This being the
case, it appears that an intellectual gulf did exist between
Clark's own conception of his relation to the territory and
the image of him held by the new settlers of Missouri. One
astute observer of the election seemed to have sensed what
really happened in the election of 1820 when he wrote,
"The opinions of a great many of the people of this territory have either not been correctly understood or a great

change has taken place in them in regard to men who have made a great nois here for some years past."[62]

In the changing political arena, some of Clark's colleagues demonstrated in their appeals to the people that they understood the values of the new order. Clark, as governor of the Missouri Territory, on the other hand, continued to conduct himself in a manner which indicated that he saw the interests of the people of Missouri as indistinguishable from the interests of the national government. Because he did so in the face of a maturing new order, many Missourians misunderstood and despised him. This attitude resulted in his political defeat in the state gubernatorial election of 1820.

VIII

Clark and the Concept of an Agrarian Indian Community

From the time of his political defeat in 1820 until his death in 1838, Clark became totally immersed in the problems of Indian affairs. It was not apparent at first that he could continue as an Indian agent after his political defeat. An ordinance in 1786 had combined the position of superintendent of Indian affairs with that of territorial governor, and, with Missouri's admission to statehood in 1821, both posts were eliminated. The need to continue the Indian superintendency was apparent, however, with the demise of the factory system and the increasingly complex problem of Indian removal. Consequently, in 1822, Congress passed a special act creating the post of superintendent of Indian affairs in St. Louis.

Clark was appointed to the position at a salary of fifteen hundred dollars a year. The stated jurisdiction of his superintendency reflected the impractical state of Indian affairs as it included "all the tribes that frequent that place [St. Louis]."[2] The vague provision of Clark's jurisdiction further indicated that the federal government saw Indian matters in a temporary and, consequently, haphazard light. Although Congress recognized the need for a more centralized and efficient Indian department by creating the post of superintendent of Indian affairs, it was not until 1834 that a serious effort was made to reorganize

Indian affairs under supervision of a permanent Indian bureau.

Upon assuming office, Clark immediately issued instructions to eighteen subordinate agents regarding the termination of the factory system. He ordered them to meet with the tribes under their direct supervision and to seek necessary treaty adjustments in all cases where a government factory had been guaranteed. He also ordered factors to deliver their remaining stock to the agents for use in negotiating new treaties.[3] This project was nearly completed by the end of 1822, but a more complex problem relating to Indian removal still awaited Clark.

Indian removal, in an informal manner, had been taking place since the beginnings of white intrusions on the North American Continent. The policy of Indian removal became formalized in 1818 when in the treaty with the Delaware Indians of Ohio and Indiana a removal clause was included. From that time, as the history of the American Indian has well documented, treaty after treaty removed the tribes of the eastern United States from their ancestral lands to areas west of the Mississippi. By 1840 virtually all the tribes east of the Mississippi had been removed to the western territories.[4]

Enlightenment-influenced Jeffersonian ideals concerning Indian assimilation clearly emerged in Clark's conceptual framework through his actions and suggestions for policy changes on Indian removal. Clark's role is extremely important because it illustrates just how much the conceptual base of Indian policy had changed from an era when it was influenced by Thomas Jefferson to later years when it was symbolized by Andrew Jackson.

Since institutional, and in some cases even rhetorical, continuity existed between the two eras of Indian policy, some historians have also assumed a continuity in basic

American conceptions of the Indian and of his proposed relationship to the rest of American society.[5]

History often unfolds on several levels of awareness. The human drama is full of examples where contemporaries have supported similar positions for very different and sometimes conflicting reasons. Because of this fact, it is difficult to point to the lack of institutional change as an indicator of the lack of intellectual change. William Clark's life is a good example of this phenomenon.

Many of the same people who had castigated Clark as a political figure applauded him in life and eulogized him after death as an effective administrator of Indian affairs, in spite of the fact that he viewed Indian policy from the same conceptual base as he did territorial politics. The answer to this puzzling twist of fate rests squarely on Clark's performance in keeping with his Jeffersonian values. As a political figure, Clark's conceptual framework was made visible and was acted out in a manner that directly affected citizens on a very tangible level. As an administrator of Indian affairs, his conceptual framework had no occasion to be made visible, for he supported, from 1820 until his death, a policy of Indian removal, a course that coincided with the interests of the frontier dwellers.

But while Clark and the frontiersmen favored the goal of Indian removal, their conceptions of what that program would accomplish differed greatly. With the discontinuance of the factory system in 1821 and with little congressional interest in increasing personnel for effective control against the harmful effects of illicit trading practices, it seems that Clark saw his hopes for assimilation of the Indian placed in jeopardy. If Clark's conceptual framework is considered along with the rapid pace of westward settlement and the lack of effective control in the Indian fur trade, it is evident that he came to view Indian removal as the only hope for Indian assimilation. From this perspective it seems clear that Clark, unlike the frontier settler and Andrew Jackson, had a definite plan in mind that would, for the societal whole, increase the availability of good farm lands, eliminate a threat to peace on the frontier, and incorporate the Indian into American life. This, then, becomes the subtle distinction between Clark's Jeffersonian concepts which featured an interdependence of societal units and the conceptual framework of a later mentality symbolized by Jackson wherein all units competed with one another for priority.

It seems that the major stumbling block faced by historians of American Indian policy is their failure to effectively incorporate the intellectual orientation and change of early and later Indian policy makers within the realm of economic self-interest and institutional structures. Clark's career, which began under Jefferson and ended under Jackson, suggests that historians might take the Enlightenment rhetoric of the early policy makers and give it serious consideration in light of the actual implementation of Indian policy, again from the perspective of the policy maker. A comparison on a conceptual level of the programs proposed by Andrew Jackson and William Clark demonstrates this course.

In the winter of 1825–26, federal officials asked Clark for recommendations on Indian policy. In his response one continues to find a Jeffersonian Enlightenment concept of the Indian. In 1826, Clark declared that the government had a duty in regard to the Indians:

The events of the last two or three wars, from General Wayne's campaign, in 1794, to the end of the operations against the southern tribes, in 1818, have entirely changed our position with regard to the Indians. Before those events, the tribes nearest our settlements were a formidable and terrible enemy; since then, their power has been broken, their warlike spirit subdued, and themselves sunk into objects of pity and commiseration. While strong and hostile, it has been our obvious policy to weaken them; now that they are weak and harmless, and most of their lands fallen into our hands, justice and humanity require us to cherish and befriend them. To teach them to live in houses, to raise grain and stock, to plant orchards, to set up landmarks, to divide their possessions, to establish laws for their government, to get the rudiments of common learning, such as reading, writing, and ciphering, are the first steps toward improving their condition. But, to take these steps with effect, it is necessary that previous measures of great magnitude should be accomplished; that is, that the tribes now within the limits of the States and Territories should be removed to a country beyond those limits, where they could rest in peace, and enjoy in reality the perpetuity of the lands on which their buildings and improvements would be made.[6]

To Clark's way of thinking, which was still oriented toward assimilation, the manner in which annuities were paid to the tribes would greatly affect their chances for improvement.

In agreeing upon the amount, I have preferred a limit to a permanent annuity; I conceived the former to be more valuable to the Indians and to the Federal Government.

An annuity forever must of course be small; and the dividend to each individual becomes so inconsiderable, that the Government confers no favor by bestowing it, and the Indians enjoy no benefit by receiving it; it is, in fact, received with contempt instead of gratitude, and the Government is burdened with a perpetual debt, the annual payment of which is doing more harm than good. And if the tribes become extinct, as has already happened in some cases of permanent annuities, then an evil of the opposite extreme is experienced; for a few individuals received the whole and become pensioners on Government, without rendering any service in return.[7]

Clark's statement clarifies several points. He was still thinking in terms of making the Indian an integral part of American life. He showed a deep concern for balancing the Indians' interests with those of the national government. Consequently, the larger annuity would serve to give the Indian enough capital to own land and make improvements. In a Jeffersonian sense, the whole process of owning and working land would provide the environmental impetus for assimilation into American society. Clark saw a balanced justice in a limited annuity: the government escaped a perpetual obligation, and the Indian received a larger, immediate grant. The limited annuity would benefit the Indian and eventually, like the white yeoman farmer, offer a service to the nation-state and himself. From the vantage point of hindsight, Clark's notions of Indian assimilation seem utter nonsense, but this is unimportant for we must deal with him in his own terms.

To be sure, rhetoric of a seemingly similar nature can be found on the part of Andrew Jackson. For example, in his second annual message to Congress in 1830, Jackson stated that Indian removal

. . . will separate the Indians from immediate contact with the settlements of whites; free them from the power of the

Andrew Jackson, from an engraving by Charles Phillips, after a painting by John Wesley Jarvis in 1815 *(Courtesy Library of Congress)*, (From *The Southern Indians*, by R. S. Cotterill)

States; enable them to pursue happiness in their own way and under their own rude institutions; will retard the progress of decay, which is lessening their numbers, and perhaps cause them gradually, under the protection of the Government and through the influence of good counsels, to cast off their savage habits and become an interesting, civilized, and Christian community.[8]

In terms of rhetoric, it appears that both Clark and Jackson were advocating the same policy of removing the Indian as humanely as possible. Though on the surface this seems to be an accurate assessment, on a conceptual level there was a vast difference between the two men, the distinction lying in their views on the ability of the Indian to progress. Their notions on the dynamics of change in large part provide the basis for understanding this difference.

Jackson considered the Indian inferior to the white man. On the basis of the premise, Jackson could only hope for progress in the Indian, while expecting little. He made this quite clear in his fifth annual message to Congress in 1833:

That those tribes cannot exist surrounded by our settlements and in continual contact with our citizens is certain. They have neither the intelligence, the industry, the moral habits, nor the desire of improvement which are essential to any favorable change in their condition. Established in the midst of another and a superior race, and without appreciating the causes of their inferiority of seeking to control them, they must necessarily yield to the force of circumstances and erelong disappear.[9]

Based on Jackson's assumption of the inferiority of the

Indian, that race's insistence on remaining among the whites was intolerable. If the Indian could not progress, he must be removed so as not to impede the progress of the rest of the nation. The only remaining solution, therefore, was the expedient one of removal, where the Indians could "pursue happiness in their own way and under their own rude institutions."[10] Jackson's support of Indian removal, therefore, was essentially negative, perhaps more in the vein of a reaction to a gnawing and embarrassing problem. From Jackson's perspective of the lineal order of interests in society, he understandably placed a higher priority on the interests of the dominant white settlers.

On the other hand, consider the marked difference in Clark's conception of Indian removal. Still adhering to an Enlightenment view of the Indian's ability to progress, two central elements—property ownership and an agrarian life-style—constituted his conception of Indian removal. Clark once proposed to John C. Calhoun that a thirty-year transition period be established in which the Indian would be isolated from foreign as well as domestic traders and settlers.[11]

To understand Clark's reasoning behind his advocacy of removal, it is once again necessary to recall his inherent Enlightenment values. Remembering the Lockean principles of experience and reflection as the sum total of man's being, it follows that the Indian, once exposed to the same environmental circumstances as white Americans, would after a time begin to identify with those values. When this basic Lockean notion is considered with the rest of Clark's recommendations, it becomes clear that he saw property ownership and an agrarian life as the environmental vehicles for Indian assimilation.

Clark suggested that only personnel acquainted with the Indians be employed and that they be "zealous" in the conviction that the Indian should be removed to western territories. Clark no doubt wanted people who were familiar with Indians because they would be more effective in using persuasion. Clark recognized that, in terms of assimilation, time was running out for the eastern tribes, and he wanted to get them moved before additional blood was shed. In addition, Clark proposed that suitable land be reserved for the Indians and that a sufficient number of agents be employed to assist the tribes in their emigration by supplying provisions and ammunition. Clark's most significant warning was directed at the method of removal. "Nor should they be required to move in a body, but singly, or in families as they pleased."[12] Clark recognized that the integrity of the Indians was at stake, and he wanted, in turn, to avoid the stigma of forcing Indians to move as herds of displaced people. He went on to make a passionate plea for measures to make the Indian free:

To assist them in commencing an agricultural life, by enclosing with fences an adequate portion of ground near to each village, and have it broken up with the plough, and divided into parcels for each family, and have it planted with all the common and most useful fruit-trees; also, furnish them with stock animals, and the different kinds of fowls, and assist them in the erection of permanent houses.

The condition of many tribes west of the Mississippi is the most pitiable that can be imagined. During several seasons in every year they are distressed by famine, in which many die for want of food, and during which the living child is often buried with the dead mother, because no one can spare it as much food as would sustain it through its helpless infancy. This description applies to the Sioux, Osages, and many others; but I mention those

*because they are powerful tribes, and live near our bor-
ders, and my official station enables me to know the exact
truth. It is in vain to talk to people in this condition about
learning and religion. They want a regular supply of food,
and, until that is obtained, the operations of the mind must
take the instinct of mere animals, and be confined to ward-
ing off hunger and cold.*[13]

Clark also advocated the establishment of common
schools to educate all Indian children in the rudimentary
levels as opposed to educating a few to college level. He
further warned against abuses in the employment of the
Indian education fund. A specific plan for education
should be drawn up with specific regulations for personnel
who would be accountable for its implementation. Once
established, the plan should be carried out by supervisors
and teachers who would be subject to frequent and rigorous examinations. Initially the education funds were set
aside from the regular annuity. A treaty with the Kaskaskia
Indians in 1803 began a policy of contributing specific
funds for the establishment of schools and educational
needs for the Indians. A problem with this system was that
the term "education" implied a broad spectrum of activities, including provisions of such things as agricultural
implements and domestic animals. In addition, the program, while federally funded, was usually operated by
religious missionary groups.[14] Clark, therefore, was proposing that specific educational funds be used for the
intellectual training of the Indians and that such funds
should be closely supervised by secular administrators
chosen for their expertise in Indian matters.

As another goal, Clark hoped to instill in the Indian the
notion of submission to a civil authority. He felt this could
be achieved by gathering tribes of the same language in

one vicinity and by placing over them a competent agent who would represent the executive power. He believed that such a move would keep chieftains from starting wars for supremacy. He further recommended that other positions within the Indian government be filled by "the different contending chiefs."[15]

Clark's final recommendation was an articulation of his earlier views on the nature of annuities. He reiterated his advocacy of larger temporary annuities, but this time he clearly stated what he felt such an action would accomplish:

It is property which has raised the character of the southern tribes. Roads and travellers through their country, large annuities, and large sums for land from the United States, and large presents to chiefs, have enabled them to acquire slaves, cattle, hogs, and horses; and these have enabled them to live independently, and to cultivate their minds and keep up their pride. . . .[16]

Here is it plainly seen that Clark was applying Jeffersonian political theory to bring about Indian assimilation. The interrelation of an agrarian environment with property ownership free from the damaging effects of the white trader would, in time, produce a responsible citizen much in the Jeffersonian image. Clark plainly expressed great faith in the almost mechanistic interrelationship of an agrarian environment and property ownership as means of producing an assimilated Indian.

Clark, then, in practice demonstrated an Enlightenment view of the development of civilizations, the premise of which is that all civilizations are a part of a universal civilization and therefore unlike only in their stages of development. This is why Enlightenment thinkers such as Benjamin Barton were so interested in comparing American civilization to other civilizations of the world:

... the physical differences between nations are but incon-
siderable, and history informs us, that civilization has
been constantly preceded by barbarity and rudeness. ...
The Americans are not, as some writers have supposed,
specifically different from the Persians, and other im-
proved nations of Asia. The inference from this discovery
is interesting and important. We learn that the Americans
are susceptible of improvement.[17]

Clark, too, in his recommendations concerning the
Indian, seems to have recognized Indian civilization not
as ultimately separate with its own origins, but as a part
of the universal body of man and consequently subject to
"progress" with a change in environment. Once this Enlightenment reasoning is understood, it is easy to see why
Clark had such respect for the Indians; in effect, he and
they belonged to the same body of universal mankind,
existing only in a different stage.

Clark's conception of Indian removal, therefore, was
unlike Jackson's. It was not negative and reactive, but
positive and schematic. In Clark's rhetoric the workings
of the Enlightenment mind are evident. Through the
mechanical manipulation of environmental factors, Clark
felt that he was providing all of the vehicles—education,
property ownership, agrarian life-style, notions of government—necessary to achieve a definite and prescribed
result. Clark even went so far as to describe the process
of change that would take place in the Indian as he progressed in Enlightenment fashion from one stage of civilization to another. In discussing the transition, he stated:

The period of danger to him [the Indian] is that in which
he ceases to be a hunter, from the extinction of game, and
before he gets the means of living from the produce of

flocks and agriculture. In this transit from the hunter to the farming state, he degenerates from a proud and independent savage to the condition of a beggar, drunkard and thief; neglecting his family, suffering for food and clothes, and living the life of a mere animal. To counteract the dangers of this is indispensable; and, to furnish these, the permanent annuities should be commuted into a gross sum, payable in equal annual parts, for a moderate term of years; and the women and children, upon whom the Labor of cultivating the ground devolves, should be assisted in making fences, to which their own means and strength are inadequate; also, in planting orchards, and instructed in raising cotton, and in spinning and weaving it into cloth, and making it up into garments. Small mills should be built, and a miller provided, to save the women from the labor of pounding the corn; useful mechanics employed to make their ploughs, carts, wheels, hoes, axes, &c., and for the purpose of teaching the young Indians how to use and make them.[18]

Truly, Clark's plans sought to create a Jeffersonian agrarian Indian community in the western territories, one whose future goals and aspirations would be indistinguishable from the rest of America. If successful, Clark would have attained the integration of the interests of various components of early nineteenth-century America—the territorial settler, the Indian, and the American nation-state. The apparent inconsistency in Jeffersonian Indian policy and Clark's role in Indian removal lies not in the minds of Thomas Jefferson and William Clark but in the minds of the twentieth-century historians who interpret early Indian policy void of its Enlightenment context.

Most of Clark's statements which have been cited were

made at the time he was in Washington advising officials on Indian policy. When he returned to St. Louis, the reality of the Indian situation awaited him. At that time he wrote to Thomas McKenney, superintendent of Indian affairs in Washington, reporting the grim conditions of the emigrating tribes and asking tactfully for the federal government to give more attention to their needs.

> *I must request you to draw the attention of the Secretary of War, to the moving, or Emigrating Indians; who are continually coming on to this side of the Mississippi. Those that have come on, and not permanently settled (many of them) are scattered for the purpose of procuring subsistance, and frequent complaints are made against them, by the white People; and considerable expense incured in reconciling the difficulties. No means is under my controll to prevent further difficulties, until funds are placed in my hands for the purpose. . . .*
>
> *I have taken upon myself to give some partial assistance to those Bands, who I was compelled to notice. —The Tribes on this side of the Mississippi are wretched and moving from place to place—. . . .*
>
> *The distresses of the Indians of this Superintendency are so great and extensive, and complaints so frequent, it is, and has been impossible for me to report them. I therefore have taken upon myself a great deal, in acting as I thought best; I have not troubled the government with numerous occurrences, which they could not remedy.*[19]

The turmoil created by the migration of tribes to the West and the constant pressure for action from men like Clark made it apparent to Washington officials that a major reorganization was necessary in the implementation of Indian policy. In 1828, Clark was once again called to

Washington, this time to draw up a bill in co-operation with Lewis Cass for the organization of an Indian department.[20] In accepting the invitation, Clark made several preliminary comments to the secretary of war indicating the kinds of proposals he would bring to Washington:

> . . . *from my own experience it would appear that the interests of the Government, as well as the dictates of humanity & justice require a revision of our Laws & regulations on the Subject of Indians. . . . The Laws regulating Indian intercourse are not sufficiently explicit & consistent to punish the various descriptions of offences which arise within & without the Country. To inforce the regulations of the Department such as may arise under various Indian Treaties I am decidedly of the opinion that a general system of regulation similar to those which govern the administration of the several branches of the military service might be advantageously adapted for the guidance of our Indian relations hereafter to exist between the Government & them under which whose scattered & miserable remnants of the people of America, could be benefited by the just & benevolent views of the Government.*[21]

Their work completed on February 9, 1829, Cass and Clark submitted a lengthy bill consisting of fifty-six sections. These placed greater emphasis on efficient organization of the administrative structure of the Indian department than on any marked changes in policy. We need not discuss here conceptual differences between Cass and Clark, since their bill dealt mainly with administrative matters on which the views of the two were quite similar. Cass and Clark both faced similar problems in carrying out government Indian policy, and both saw improved regulations as the best means to solve those problems.[22] The bill called for the appointment of an Indian commissioner to head an independent department, thus relieving the secretary of war of the responsibility of Indian affairs. In addition, the bill outlined explicit responsibilities of officials in the Indian department.

The Cass-Clark bill also suggested some modifications in policy, especially as it applied to the determination of boundary lines of Indian lands. Because of the chaotic nature of Indian migration, it was felt that boundary lines had to be more flexible in order to change with the crowded conditions as more tribes moved west. Perhaps the most significant change in the proposed bill was one giving Indian agents greater discretionary power to enforce rigid regulations governing the granting of trade licenses. In addition, the bill specifically prohibited all liquor in the Indian country except that used by a trading party itself. The bill also sought to remove from the president's hands power to grant exemptions to the liquor prohibition clause. Finally, the Cass-Clark bill contained the stiff proviso, first adopted in the regulations of 1816, that all persons entering Indian country, even in a nontrading capacity, had to have special passports.[23]

In summary, the bill attempted to centralize authority, to clearly define the limits of authority, and to efficiently disburse funds to the Indian tribes. The bill also provided for standardized accounting procedures to facilitate investigation of possible waste and fraud.

When Clark left Washington in the spring of 1829, he was aware that Congress would not act on his bill. Since he had actually experienced the grim state of Indian affairs on the frontier, he had less confidence than others in the chances of achieving a humane Indian policy that would serve the interests of both the Indian and the government.

In addition to rejecting the Cass-Clark bill, Congress showed signs of giving less attention to Indian matters. On March 10, 1829, Clark was informed by the secretary of war that "the present state of funds of the Indian Department requires the most rigid economy in all the disbursements which the officers of that Department are called upon to make. You are earnestly desired to reduce the expenditures of your Superintendency to the lowest possible amount. . . ."[24]

While the government was decreasing its emphasis on Indian affairs, conditions in the West made it apparent that such action was not warranted. From Clark's perspective this was the case not only for humanitarian reasons but also for reasons more reminiscent of the pre-War of 1812 days when the Americans and British were locked in an economic struggle for the Northwest. The manner and importance of trade in this struggle has already been emphasized. Although the agricultural settler replaced the mercantile capitalist as the important factor in advancing the American empire in the early nineteenth century, Clark remained locked in a mercantile frame of mind which persisted to stress the dangers of the British trader and the need for Americans to maintain an effective deterrent.

Clark's mercantile frame of mind concerning the western territories can be seen in his 1831 report to the federal government on the condition of the fur trade. In assessing the matter, Clark referred, ironically, to his hated enemy, the British trader, in suggesting methods to improve the fur trade and eliminate its bad effects on the Indian:

In elucidating the present conditions of the Fur Trade on the frontiers of the States, it will be seen to lie under many disadvantages; some of which, and not the least of them

*maybe referred to Extraneous causes which altho they
perhaps cannot be immediately removed, yet can be
checked by a countervailing policy on the part of the
Government. I allude to the preference which the Indians
themselves have always shewn and still continue to shew
the English:—a preference which I have never been able
to account for on other grounds, than by viewing it as the
effect of an intercourse, the manner of which has been
prescribed, controlled, and Enforced by their Government
which has Executed its Laws & regulations in this respect
with perhaps a rather despotic, yet Salutary sway.*[25]

Clark pointed to the rigid control which the British
exerted over their traders as a reason for their success.
Hence, Clark's view in 1831 had not changed since his
1815 proposal for a large American fur company under
government regulation to compete with the British.

Clark's sentiments for a more active role by the federal
government in the fur trade, however, were in direct
contrast to the mood of the nation in 1831, a mood which
increasingly stressed private enterprise free from the
regulation of the national government. Clark's emphasis
on the role of the government in the fur trade had humanitarian implications for the Indian as well in that it could
help curb illicit trading practices.

Competition among traders for furs on the American
side of the Canadian border led them to employ liquor
as a means of attracting the Indian's business and also of
reducing his powers of bargaining skillfully. Although
liquor had long been prohibited in such trade, the regulation was commonly ignored. In 1831, one of Clark's
agents estimated that only one out of a hundred gallons
of liquor taken into Indian country was covered by a per-
mit from Clark.[26] In discussing the transport of liquor

into Indian territory, Clark noted that his enforcement policy had changed. Initially he had not inspected the goods of traders going into Indian country, taking their word as to the amount of liquor they carried. In 1831, however, he stated:

> ... I have received information on the Subject; and from such a source as to place the matter beyond a doubt and to convince that the priviledge of taking Whiskey for the use of the Boatmen has been abused: that instead thereof and for the purposes specified alcohol had been taken which it seems (after being reduced) has been furnished to the Indians by the gallon & Keg.
>
> As those Traders have evinced so little good faith ... I shall conceive it my bound duty to recommend the total & entire prohibition of this article in the Indian Country under any pretence or for any purpose whatever.[27]

Curbing liquor in the fur trade was an almost impossible task. In his 1831 report Clark specifically pointed out the difficulty of prosecuting a trader who violated the liquor provision:

> I would answer, that the institution of a suit on a trader's bond, with such an object in view, would be considered as a mere farce; as past experience fully shows that, in order to [have] a successful prosecution, there are many things to be proven before a court having cognizance of the offence, which would not occur at the time to the witness testifying. It would prove nothing that he should have witnessed the process of reducing the alcohol in the trader's house and the putting it into casks; that he should have seen the liquor drawn from these same casks, put into kegs, and delivered to Indians, who conveyed the

*same to their camps, which, after a few hours, exhibited
a scene of the most frightful drunkenness:—he must be
able to testify that he has tasted this liquor, and found it
to be spiritous, in order to produce a conviction. And
when it is considered that an individual seeking to qualify
himself by these means to produce the conviction of the
traders, would at once arouse suspicions which might
result in the most serious consequences to himself, the
difficulty attending it may be easily imagined.*[28]

This problem which confronted frontier Indian officials
was not a new discovery. In 1808, for example, a government agent confiscated the furs of an unlicensed trader,
only to be personally countersued by the trader for his
public actions.

On March 30, 1834, Clark's earlier pleas for changes in
Indian policy and regulation finally achieved some effect
through the passage of two congressional acts. The Indian
Trade and Intercourse Act and the Indian Reorganization
Act largely incorporated provisions from earlier bills but
also reflected recommendations made through the years
by Indian officials, including those of Cass and Clark in
1829. Much like the earlier Cass-Clark bill, the 1834 legis-
lation sought to tighten trade regulations and curb liquor
abuses through stricter and more efficient enforcement.[29]

In retrospect, however, it can be seen that the acts of
1834 did too little too late to curb the abuses perpetrated
on the Indian by the white settler whose appetite for new
land was insatiable. Clark would live only four more
years, and had he lived much beyond 1838 he could not
have realistically entertained his hopes for an Indian
pastoral community in the West which would, according
to anachronistic Jeffersonian ideals, peaceably assimilate
the Indian into American life. The lure of western land

proved too much of an economic temptation to white settlers imbued with the idea that they could fulfill America's divine destiny by occupying virgin soils at the greatest possible speed.

While the prevailing sentiment of the nation was joy at the submission of the Indian, Clark expressed his frustrations over the situation in a letter to an old friend from another age, Thomas Jefferson:

In my present situation of Superintendent of Indian Affairs, it would afford me Pleasure to be enabled to——the conditions of these unfortunate people placed under my charge, Knowing as I do their retchedness and their rapid decline[.] It is to be lamented that the deplorable Situation of the Indians do not receive more of the human feelings of the nation.[30]

Epilogue

On August 31, 1838, the *Missouri Republican* announced that William Clark "was dangerously ill and late yesterday evening was not expected to survive many hours."[1] The next day, on September 1, 1838, he died at the age of sixty-eight.

The last two decades of Clark's life were marked by tragedy and frustration. In 1821, Clark married Harriet Radford, a cousin of his deceased first wife, only to have her pass away a decade later on Christmas Day, 1831. In that decade he also lost three children: a seven-year old daughter, Mary Margaret, died in 1821; an infant son of ten months passed away in 1827; and in 1831 his thirteen-year old son, John Julius, died.[2]

These last years were also marked by financial insecurity in the face of his earnest desire to educate his children. In 1833 one of Clark's sons, William Preston, wrote to his brother George Rogers, "you must not expect a fortune from your father's estate, he is using every exertion to give his children an education and will have little left to divide among them. . . ."[3]

William Preston's remark might at first seem puzzling since Clark's last will and testament shows that he owned a considerable amount of land. The bulk of his holdings were located in southern Indiana and northwest Kentucky,

Harriet Kennerly Radford Clark, from portrait by Chester Harding, 1828? *(Courtesy Mary Kearny Cobb)*, (From *Persimmon Hill: A Narrative of Old St. Louis and the Far West*, by William Clark Kennerly)

acreage worth approximately twenty-three thousand dollars which he had inherited from his brother, George Rogers Clark. In addition, he owned a considerable amount of land and property in St. Louis. It could be estimated that in St. Louis alone he held between seventy and eighty thousand dollars worth of property.[4] When examined more closely, this development provides further evidence of a conceptual framework conceived early in his life. Despite Clark's apparently wealthy economic status, on more than one occasion he complained of the small amount of money he had to raise his family. It must be remembered that land was not necessarily held for speculative purposes. Indeed, it was a measure of an eighteenth-century Virginian to see much more security in land holding for its own virtue than in the fluid capital worth of the land. This is an important distinction between a large landowner and a large land speculator.

Clark was not completely free of the speculative mania, however, for he attempted to capitalize on his five thousand acres by plotting a town at the confluence of the Tennessee and Ohio rivers. Clark named the town after a Chickasaw Indian friend, Chief Paduke. An advertisement in the May 3, 1827 issue of the *Missouri Republican* offered the lots for sale:

PA-DU-CAH
The undersigned has laid off about 100 acres in a town called PA-DU-CAH, in lots of suitable size, which will be sold to the highest bidders, at the place, on Saturday the 26th day of May next and continued from day to day, until as many lots are sold as may be deemed necessary for the commencement of a town. . . .[5]

Clark never again mentioned Paducah or how the venture

paid off. He seems not to have realized any immediately spectacular return on his Paducah venture, however, as its growth was slow. It was incorporated as a village of only 105 people three years after Clark launched the project. Paducah served mainly as a transshipment point for steam traffic on the Missouri, Mississippi, and Ohio rivers. The town had little local industry until the mid-nineteenth century when a lumbering industry sprang up there. By 1845, Paducah had a population of 1,500, indicating a steady but unspectacular growth.[6]

In any event, William Clark's will confirms the fact that he liquidated very little of his holdings; his legacy to his sons consisted of land and property valued in excess of $120,000.[7] It is truly a remarkable phenomenon that Clark, living in the midst of the speculative mania of the early nineteenth century, liquidated so little of his vast holdings. This provides yet another clue to Clark's unchanged intellectual framework.

Missourians afforded Clark great respect and honor following his death. The *Missouri Republican* eulogized him by recalling his many accomplishments, citing the Lewis and Clark expedition, his role as governor of the Missouri Territory, and especially his role as superintendent of Indian affairs and the affection accorded him by the Indian. The eulogy ended by stating that

He was sixty-eight years of age when he died, and was probably the oldest American settler residing in St. Louis. Through a long, eventful and useful life, he has filled the various stations of a citizen and officer with such strict integrity and in so affable and mild a manner, that, at that day of his death, malice nor destraction had not a blot to fix upon the fair scroll which the history of his well-spent life leaves as a rich and estimable legacy to his children, and the numerous friends who now mourn his death.[8]

The *Saturday News* said of him:

GENERAL WILLIAM CLARK

A long personal acquaintance with and a knowledge of the character of General Clark, enables us to pronounce that which will be affirmed by all who have known the deceased, that he was more faultless, and more virtuous, than almost any man whoever held so conspicuous a station for so long a time.[9]

Clark was buried in the family vault on the farm of his nephew, John O'Fallon, following the largest funeral that St. Louis had seen to that date.[10] The following description from the *Missouri Saturday News* gives an idea of the esteem and affection felt for Clark at his death:

The carriages of mourners followed the remains of the venerated General and were preceded by his horse in full caparison, which was led by one of his household servants, whose humid eye told how deeply he lamented the loss of his paternal and indulgent master.

The long train of carriages filled with many of our most esteemable citizens, were followed by a much greater number of public vehicles, which held a place in the procession not with empty *show, but filled with citizens who cherished the most devoted affection and sincere respect for the deceased. The procession was closed with gentlemen on horseback, extending the line more than a mile in length.*

When the head of the procession approached within a short distance of the cemetery, the minute guns com-

*menced firing and continued until the hearse reached
its final destination. Here, when the mortal remains had
been deposited in their resting place and the Masonic
rites performed, the burial service of the Episcopal Church
was pronounced over the deceased by the reverend Mr.
Mainard.*

*The concluding honors of war closed the funeral solem-
nities, and the volleys of musketry which were discharged
drew responsive echo from the undulating surface of the
surrounding country. From the point where this illustrious citizen was interred, near to one of those artificial
mounds which cover the ashes of some great red chief, the
confluence of the Father of the Waters with the mighty
current of the Missouri, or mad water, can be observed,
together with the white cliffs beyond them. This position
he had chosen for the repose of his ashes as best suited to
his elevated fancy, and where in life time his adventurous
enthusiasm could take in a wide discursive range.*[11]

The irony of Clark's death was that Missourians had
adorned and elegantly buried an image of William Clark,
an image that depicted a man dedicated to his country,
dutifully carrying out its policies without any particular
vision of his own. The real Clark was not known to them
because his vision was not of their age. An ordered, pastoral society, red and white, respectful of its laws and leaders, was anachronistic in an age when change and growth
were bywords for progress. Only once did Missourians
see the real vision of William Clark and that was during
the years 1813 to 1820 when he was the political leader of
the territory. In those years they despised what he stood
for and rejected him in the most bitter terms. On the other
hand, as an administrative figure deeply involved in Indian removal, Clark was applauded because, according to

the prevailing mentality, the removal of the dreaded Indian was the removal of an obstacle to progress. Clark remained popular to his death and beyond because his vision of an eventual Indian pastoral community alongside white settlements never materialized, and the most obtuse could recognize that the Indian was gone.

Notes

CHAPTER I

1. Scholars of learning behavior are generally united in their emphasis on the impact of learning in the early years of life. They point to the period of early childhood as critical to the establishment in the child of the mores of a given society. "The traditions, folkways, and mores of a society weave their subtle fabric around the infant from the moment of birth—and, indeed, even before birth: Patterns of behavior in the broad society as well as in specific subcultural groups, impinge upon the infant and shape his deepest responses to the environment into which he is born." From Edith W. King and August Kerber, *The Sociology of Early Childhood Education*, 43. Earlier studies by C. H. Cooley, *Human Nature and the Social Order*; and G. H. Mead, *Mind, Self and Society*, Part III; and Jean Piaget, *The Language and Thought of the Child*, combined with more recent works by Erik Erikson, *Childhood and Society*; and Fred I. Greenstein, *Children and Politics*; and David Easton and Robert D. Hess, "The Child's Political World," *Midwest Journal of Political Science*, Vol. VI (1962), 229–46; and Yehudi A. Cohen (ed.), *Social Structure and Personality: A Casebook*, New York, 1961 all stress the importance of experiences during the first five years in developing lasting values. This, of course, is not to discount individuality of development which is accountable to a great number of variables, including family structure, social organizations, peer groups, and media impact. Studies helpful in pursuing this line of thinking include Frederick Elkin, *The Child and Society: The Process of Socialization*; and Mary Ellen Goodman, *The Individual and Culture*. My purpose in developing this body of literature is to demonstrate that there are viable reasons for stressing the longevity of Enlightenment thinking in Clark's life, while at the same time recognizing the impact of individual personality traits as well as circumstances and events peculiar to his life.

2. Ernst Cassirer, *The Philosophy of the Enlightenment* (trans. by Fritz C. A. Loella and James P. Pettegrove), and Gerald R. Cragg, *Rea-*

son and Authority in the Eighteenth Century, were most helpful in understanding Enlightenment religious views. A good view of Enlightenment political and social orientation is Lester Crocker, *Nature and Culture: Ethical Thought in the French Enlightenment.* The question of whether or not the Enlightenment existed in America is discussed by Peter Gay, "The Enlightenment," in *The Comparative Approach to American History* (ed. by C. Vann Woodward). The student interested in the Enlightenment should also consult Charles Frankel, *The Faith of Reason*; R. V. Sampson, *Progress in the Age of Reason*; Lester G. Crocker, *An Age of Crisis: Man and World in Eighteenth Century French Thought*; and Francis X. J. Coleman, *The Aesthetic Thought of the French Enlightenment.* For a specific treatment of the American Enlightenment, see Peter Gay's bibliography at the end of his essay in *The Comparative Approach to American History.*

3. William Clark Memorandum Book, 1798, frontispiece, Western Historical Manuscripts Collection, University of Missouri, Columbia, Missouri. (Hereafter cited as WHMC.)

4. Cassirer, *Philosophy of the Enlightenment*, vii.

5. A mercantile capitalist was essentially a trader-swapper type who sought to control his environment through diversification of function and efficient administration. He had simultaneous command of wholesaling, retailing, transportation, storage, communication, and banking. He attempted to diminish the risk factor of his enterprises by entering into temporary joint-venture agreements. He often sought privileges from the central government, usually in the form of monopolies. To sustain him in this end, he much preferred a strong central government to independent local control. In return, the central government could expect his aid in exploration and colonization. See N. S. B. Gras, *Business and Capitalism: An Introduction to Business History*, 74–90, 133–58 *passim.*

6. Eli F. Heckscher, *Mercantilism* (trans. by Mendel Shapiro, ed. by E. F. Söderlund), II, 328.

7. For a further discussion of territorial expansion and administration, see Howard Lamar, *Dakota Territory, 1861–1889: A Study of Frontier Politics*; Richard W. Van Alstyne, *The Rising American Empire*; and Jack Eblen, *The First and Second United States Empires: Governors and Territorial Government, 1784–1912.* These books are essentially political analyses of territorial expansion and administration. Although they make a valuable contribution to territorial history, Lamar, Van Alstyne, and Eblen fail to incorporate sufficiently America's changing conceptual framework into the political and economic story.

CHAPTER II

1. William Clark Memorandum Book, 1798, frontispiece, WHMC.

2. John Francis McDermott (ed.), *The Western Journals of Washington Irving*, 81–82.

3. John Flagg, *The Far West, 1836–37*, XXVI, Part I of *Early Western Travels, 1748–1846* (ed. by Reuben Gold Thwaites), 258–59.

4. William Clark to Edmund Clark, December 25, 1814, Clark Family Papers, Filson Club, Louisville, Kentucky, folder 1.

5. William Clark to Meriwether Lewis, March 11, 1807, Clark Papers, Missouri Historical Society-Jefferson Memorial, St. Louis, Missouri. (Hereafter cited as MHS-JM.)

6. William Hayden English, *Conquest of the Country Northwest of the River Ohio 1778–1783, Life of Gen. George Rogers Clark*, I, 30–37; R. C. Ballard Thruston, "Some Recent Findings Regarding the Ancestry of General George Rogers Clark," *The Filson Club History Quarterly*, Vol. IX (January, 1935), 1–34. It is difficult to trace the genealogy of the Clark family because fire has destroyed nearly all of the records of King and Queen County and Caroline County, Virginia. The four oldest Clark children were born in King and Queen County: Jonathan, August 1, 1750; George Rogers, November 19, 1752; Ann, July 14, 1755; and John, September 15, 1757. The remainder of the Clark children were born in Caroline County, Virginia: Richard, July 6, 1760; Edmund, September 25, 1762; Lucy, September 15, 1765; Elizabeth, February 11, 1768; William, August 1, 1770; and Frances, 1773.

7. Richard Beale Davis, *Intellectual Life in Jefferson's Virginia 1790–1830*, 6–7.

8. William Clark Kennerly as told to Elizabeth Russell, *Persimmon Hill: A Narrative of Old St. Louis and the Far West*, 6–7; James Alton James, *The Life of George Rogers Clark*, 2.

9. Kennerly, *Persimmon Hill*, 7.

10. Davis, *Jefferson's Virginia*, 6–7.

11. "Donald Robertson's School, King and Queen County Virginia, 1758–1769," *Virginia Magazine of History*, Vol. XXXIII (April, 1925), 194–98; (July, 1925), 288–92; Vol. XXXIV (April, 1926), 141–48; (July, 1926), 232–36.

12. Davis, *Jefferson's Virginia*, 35, citing Irving Brant, *James Madison the Virginia Revolutionist 1751–1780*, 60.

13. *Ibid.*, 98, citing Brant, *James Madison*, 60.

14. Jonathan Clark Papers, Draper Collection, State Historical Society of Wisconsin, Madison, Wisconsin, Microfilm 2L69.

15. William Clark Memorandum Book, 1798, frontispiece, WHMC.

16. Davis, *Jefferson's Virginia*, 178. Davis synthesizes from Edward T. Martin, *Thomas Jefferson: Scientist*, 30–66.

17. Davis, *Jefferson's Virginia*, 8–25; 387–434, *passim*; Charles S. Sydnor, *Gentlemen Freeholders*, 13–99, *passim*. (Later edition published as *American Revolutionaries in the Making: Political Practices In Washington's Virginia*.)

18. Francis B. Heitman, *Historical Register of Officers of the Continental Army During the War of the Revolution, April 1775 to December 1783*, 157; English, *Conquest Northwest of the River Ohio*, I, 38; Kennerly, *Persimmon Hill*, 8.

19. Kennerly, *Persimmon Hill*, 8.

20. *Ibid.*, 5–6.

21. Ludie Kinkead, "How the Parents of George Rogers Clark Came to Kentucky in 1784–1785," *The Filson Club History Quarterly*, Vol. III (October, 1928), 1–4; Reuben Gold Thwaites, "William Clark: Soldier, Explorer, Statesman," *Missouri Historical Society Collections*, Vol. II (October, 1906), 6; Temple Bodley, *George Rogers Clark, His Life and Public Services*, 239.

22. Ray Allen Billington, *Westward Expansion: A History of the American Frontier*, 221–45; Merrill Jensen, *The New Nation: A History of the United States During the Confederation 1781–1789*, 6–27, 330–45.

23. *Ibid.* Billington, *Westward Expansion*, 221–45; Jensen, *The New Nation*, 6–27, 330–45.

24. George Rogers Clark led some of the earlier missions against the tribes of the Ohio Valley, but there is no evidence that William Clark participated in those campaigns.

25. William Clark, Journal of Hardin's Campaign, August 2, 1789–March 18, 1790, William Clark Papers, MHS-JM, *passim*. Randolph C. Downes, *Council Fires on the Upper Ohio Valley 1795*, 311–12.

26. Downes, *Council Fires*, 310–38; John Bakeless, *Background to Glory: The Life of George Rogers Clark*, 315–24; John Bakeless, *Lewis and Clark: Partners in Discovery*, 30–33.

27. William Clark, Journal of Gen. Charles Scott's Campaign, May 25, 1791–June 16, 1791, William Clark Papers, MHS-JM.

28. Francis B. Heitman, *Historical Register and Dictionary of the United States Army from its Organization, September 29, 1789 to March 2, 1903*, I, 306; William Clark, Journal of General Wayne's Campaign, May 15, 1792–May 1794, William Clark Papers, MHS-JM; R. C. McGrane (ed.), "William Clark's Journal and General Wayne's Campaign," *Missouri Valley Historical Review*, Vol. I (December, 1941), 418–44.

29. Thwaites, "William Clark," *Missouri Historical Society Collections*, Vol. II (October, 1906), 6. See also William Clark's journals of the Hardin, Scott, and Wayne campaigns in William Clark Papers, MHS-JM.

30. Bakeless, *Partners in Discovery*, 40.

31. Anthony Wayne to Secretary of War, August 14, 1794, *American State Papers: Military Affairs*, IV, 490; William Clark, Report to Major General Wayne, November 4, 1795, William Clark Papers, MHS-JM.

32. William Clark, Journal of Wayne's Campaign, May 12–13, 1794, William Clark Papers, MHS-JM.

33. William Clark to Jonathan Clark, May 25, 1794, Jonathan Clark Papers, Draper Collection, 2L33, State Historical Society of Wisconsin, Madison, Wisconsin. (Hereafter cited as SHSW.)

34. Thomas Boyd, *Mad Anthony Wayne*, 334–35; James Hyde Preston, *A Gentleman Rebel: Mad Anthony Wayne*, 291–308.

35. Bakeless, *Partners in Discovery*, 46–47, citing the Simcoe Papers, II, 222–23, *Michigan Pioneer and Historical Collections*, Vol. XXIV (1895), 659–60.

36. William Clark to Edmund Clark, November 25, 1794, Jonathan Clark Papers, Draper Collection, 2L36, SHSW.

37. William Clark to Jonathan Clark, November 25, 1794, *ibid.*, 1L37.

38. James, *George Rogers Clark*, 459–60; William Clark to Jonathan Clark, July 30, 1799, Jonathan Clark Papers, Draper Collection, 2L52, SHSW.

39. Bakeless, *Background to Glory*, 327–28; Bodley, *George Rogers Clark: Life and Services*, 229–30; James, *George Rogers Clark*, 417–18.

40. *Ibid.*

41. William Clark to Edmund Clark, August 18, 1797, Jonathan Clark Papers, Draper Collection, 2L45, SHSW.

42. Bakeless, *Background to Glory*, 337; James, *George Rogers Clark*, 452–58.

43. Bakeless, *Background to Glory*, 331–32, 335; Bodley, *George Rogers Clark: Life and Services*, 359.

44. Bakeless, *Background to Glory*, 337; James, *George Rogers Clark*, 457–58.

45. Will, John Clark III, July 26, 1799, William Clark Papers, MHS-JM.

46. Bakeless, *Partners in Discovery*, 68; Bodley, *George Rogers Clark: Life and Services*, 358–59; James, *George Rogers Clark*, 458.

47. Meriwether Lewis to William Clark, June 19, 1803, William Clark Papers, MHS-JM.

CHAPTER III

1. James Russell Lowell, *"The Biglow Papers," The Poetic Works of James Russell Lowell*, 252.

2. Reuben Gold Thwaites (ed.), *Original Journals of the Lewis and Clark Expedition, 1804–1806*, I, xxi–xxii; Thwaites, "William Clark," *Missouri Historical Society Collections*, Vol. II (October, 1906), 1–24; Bernard DeVoto (ed.), *The Journals of Lewis and Clark*, xxii–xxiii.

3. Paul Russell Cutright, *Lewis and Clark: Pioneering Naturalists*, is one of the most recent and valuable studies stressing the scientific goals of the Lewis and Clark expedition. The bibliography is invaluable for those interested in the scientific aspects of the mission. Another work that I have found invaluable in this area is Elijah H. Criswell, *Lewis and Clark: Linguistic Pioneers*. It should also be noted that there is a vast bibliography on the Lewis and Clark Expedition, which is not central to the focus of this study. The most recent and best source of information on the Lewis and Clark Expedition and Journals is Paul Cutright, *A History of the Lewis and Clark Journals* (Norman, 1976). Cutright's bibliography extensively covers literature on all aspects of the two explorer's careers.

4. Thomas Jefferson to George Rogers Clark, December 4, 1783, Clark Papers, MHS-JM.

5. Thwaites, "William Clark," *Missouri Historical Society Collections*, Vol. II (October, 1906), 11.

6. Thwaites (ed.), *Original Journals*, I, xxi–xxii.

7. Bernard DeVoto, "An Inference Regarding the Expedition of Lewis and Clark," *American Philosophical Society Proceedings*, Vol. XCIX (August, 1955), 189.

8. *Ibid.*, 186; Donald Jackson, "The Public Image of Lewis and Clark," *Pacific Northwest Quarterly*, Vol. LVII, No. 1 (January, 1966), 5, stresses the fact that the mission ended up costing considerably more than originally intended. He estimates an amount in excess of fifty thousand dollars.

9. DeVoto (ed.), *The Journals of Lewis and Clark*, I, xxii–xxiii.

10. *Ibid.*, I, xviii.

11. Jefferson's Instructions to Lewis, June 20, 1803, in Donald Jackson, *Letters of the Lewis and Clark Expedition: With Related Documents, 1783–1854*, 61–66.

12. *Ibid.*

13. *Ibid.*

14. Francis S. Philbrick, *The Rise of the West, 1754–1830*, 234–36.

15. Bakeless, *Partners in Discovery*, 96–97.

16. Meriwether Lewis to William Clark, June 19, 1803, William Clark Papers, MHS-JM.

17. This letter is quoted in Chapter II, see footnote 41.

18. William Clark to Meriwether Lewis, July 24, 1803, William Clark Papers, MHS-JM.

19. Thwaites (ed.), *Original Journals*, I, *passim*.

20. Bakeless, *Partners in Discovery*, 155–56.

21. Thwaites (ed.), *Original Journals*, I, *passim*.

22. Thwaites, "William Clark," *Missouri Historical Society Collections*, Vol. II (October, 1906), 7.

23. DeVoto, *The Journals of Lewis and Clark*, I, xlii–xliv.

24. Thwaites (ed.), *Original Journals*, VII, 338–39.

25. *Ibid.*, 329.

26. Elijah Harry Criswell, *Lewis and Clark: Linguistic Pioneers*, University of Missouri Studies, xv, xxiv.

27. William Clark Astronomy Notebook, 1805, WHMC.

28. Thwaites (ed.), *Original Journals*, III, 137.

29. *Ibid.*, 241. Bracketed material are Thwaites' amendations.

30. Howard C. Rice, Jr., "Jefferson's Gift of Fossils to the Museum of Natural History in Paris," *American Philosophical Society Proceedings*, Vol. XCV (December, 1951), 600.

31. Thomas Jefferson to William Clark, December 19, 1802, Thomas Jefferson Papers, Library of Congress, Washington, D.C., Vol. 173, microfilm. (Hereafter cited as LC.)

32. *Ibid.*, September 10, 1809, Vol. 188, microfilm.

33. William Clark to Thomas Jefferson, December 15, 1825, Thomas Jefferson Papers, LC, Vol. 230, microfilm.

34. J. Thomas Scharf, *History of St. Louis City and County*, I, 103; John Francis McDermott, "William Clark: Pioneer Museum Man," *Washington Academy of Sciences Journal*, Vol. XLIV (November, 1954), 370–73, *passim*.

35. Henry R. Schoolcraft, *Travels in the Central Portions of the Mississippi Valley*, 294.

36. General Marquis de Lafayette to William Clark, February 1, 1830, William Clark Papers, MHS-JM.

37. *Missouri Republican*, September 11, 1838.

38. DeVoto (ed.), *The Journals of Lewis and Clark*, I, xlvi.

39. *Ibid.*, I, xliv–l.

CHAPTER IV

1. Thomas Jefferson to Meriwether Lewis, August 21, 1808, in Clarence Edwin Carter (ed.), *Territorial Papers of the United States: The Territory of Louisiana–Missouri, 1806–1814*, XIV, 220. (Hereafter cited as *Territorial Papers.)*

2. William Clark to Edmund Clark, March 5, 1807, Jonathan Clark Papers, Draper Collection, SHSW, Microfilm 2L60; Bakeless, *Background to Glory*, 381.

3. Philbrick, *The Rise of the West, 1754–1830*, 234–52, *passim.*

4. Larry A. McFarlane, "Economic Theories Significant in the Rise of the United States Indian Factory System, 1795–1817" (M.A. thesis, University of Missouri, 1955), 105.

5. Ora Peake, *The American Factory System, 1796–1822*, 1–25, *passim*; Edgar B. Wesley, "The Government Factory System Among the Indians, 1795–1822," *Journal of Economics and Business History*, Vol. IV (May, 1932), 489–96, *passim.*

6. Thomas Jefferson to Meriwether Lewis, August 21, 1808, in Carter (ed.), *Territorial Papers*, XIV, 220.

7. Daniel Boorstin, *The Lost World of Thomas Jefferson*, 88, citing Benjamin Smith Barton, *New Views of the Origins of the Tribes and Nations of America* (second edition, Philadelphia, 1798), vf.

8. Boorstin, *Lost World*, 85–86.

9. Thomas Jefferson to Chastellux, June 7, 1785, in Julian P. Boyd (ed.), *The Papers of Thomas Jefferson*, VIII, 185–86.

10. One historian, Reginald Horsman, does note the presence of Enlightenment thinking in the formulation of early Indian policy epitomized by Thomas Jefferson. In "American Indian Policy and the Origins of Manifest Destiny," *University of Birmingham Historical Journal*, Vol. XI (December, 1968), 131, Horsman states, "this attitude was essentially one of great optimism. It did not preach an innate Indian inferiority, but rather viewed the Indian as existing at a lower state in the evolution of society and civilization." In his "Indian Policy in the Northwest," *William and Mary Quarterly*, Vol. XVIII (January, 1961), 51, Horsman hit upon the very central thesis of Jefferson's policy when he stated: "It would seem that Jefferson had come to believe that not only was the civilization of the Indian convenient for acquisition of land, but that he was also acquiring land in order to civilize the Indian."

This statement by Horsman is extremely important. It represents that aspect of the Enlightenment mind which has evaded and perplexed historians trying to penetrate the dilemmas of Jefferson's Indian policy which set humanitarian rhetoric off in direct contradiction to economic self-interest. Horseman mistakenly felt that he had solved this dilemma by simply transferring it to the conscience of Thomas Jefferson; hence, he could only conclude that Jefferson's motives were ambivalent or, at best, unrealistic. Horsman, therefore, abandons Jefferson's perception of reality and returns to his own perception of reality: "the basic object of American Indian policy in this period—the acquisition of land—was a striking success." ("Indian Policy in the Northwest," *William and Mary Quarterly*, Vol. XVIII [January, 1961], 53.) For a general treatment of this issue, see Horsman's *Expansion and the American Indian Policy*, Chapter VII, "The Ambivalence of Thomas Jefferson," 104-15.

Horsman did not penetrate the dilemma that he saw in Jefferson's Indian policy because of his assumption that one of its objects had to be more important than another. Given Horsman's assumption, it was obvious for him to conclude that land acquisition, representing the reality, far outweighed the ideal of assimilation. Yet to understand Jefferson's Indian policy, it is necessary to rid oneself of this tendency to see the interests of society in a lineal order and inevitably competing with one another for priority, as is the case in contemporary society. Jefferson's intellectual reference viewed societal interests as ideally constituting a whole, with the possibility of integrating individual interests for the common good. To be sure Jefferson recognized the conflict of interests within society and the need to regulate them. But to Jefferson there was a difference between regulating society to protect the common good and regulating society to protect individual rights.

11. Peake, *American Factory System*, 1-25, *passim*; Wesley, "Government Factory System," *Journal of Economics and Business History*, Vol. IV (May, 1932), 489-96, *passim*; Edgar B. Wesley, *Guarding the Frontier: A Study of Frontier Defense from 1815 to 1825*, 31-65, *passim*.

12. Thomas Jefferson, Communication to Congress, January 18, 1803, *American State Papers: Indian Affairs*, I, 684-85.

13. Thomas Jefferson to William Henry Harrison, February 27, 1803, in Andrew H. Lipscomb (ed.), *The Writings of Thomas Jefferson*, X, 369-70. Horsman is quick to point out, however, that although Jefferson's motives may have been humanitarian, the Indian was never allowed a choice in the matter of assimilation. Similarly, Roy Harvey Pearce exposes the inconsistencies in Jefferson's thinking between "cultural relativism and moral absolutism," indicating that Jefferson used American and European civilization as the standard for judging Indian civilization. Bernard Sheehan cites the myths of the New World as a paradise and the Indian as a Noble Savage as contributing factors for the failure of Jeffersonian policy. Neither conception was realistic and, consequently, neither was the notion of Indian assimilation within the Jeffersonian scheme. Horsman, Pearce, and Sheehan have made valuable contributions by focusing on the inconsistencies in Jeffersonian Indian policy and the reasons for its failure; however, they lend little

assistance in understanding the internal reasoning of Jefferson's policy. In other words, these scholars are not dealing with Jefferson's perception of reality, but rather with their own. See Horsman, *Expansion and the American Indian Policy, 1783-1812*, 104-14; Bernard Sheehan, "Paradise and the Noble Savage in Jeffersonian Thought," *William and Mary Quarterly*, Vol. XXVI (July, 1969), 327-59; Roy Harvey Pearce, *The Savages of America: A Study of the Indian and the Idea of Civilization*, 94 (later edition published as *Savagism and Civilization: A Study of the Indian and the American Mind*).

14. McFarlane, "Economic Theories" (M.A. thesis, University of Missouri, 1955), 109-12.

15. *Ibid.*, 113.

16. Peake, *American Factory System*, 1-25, *passim*; Wesley, "Government Factory System," *Journal of Economic and Business History*, Vol. IV (May, 1932), 489-96, *passim*.

17. Wesley, "Government Factory System," *Journal of Economic and Business History*, Vol. IV (May, 1932), 493.

18. William Clark to Secretary of War, June 1, 1807, in Carter (ed.), *Territorial Papers*, XIV, 126.

19. William Clark to Secretary of War, September 23, 1808, *ibid.*, 226.

20. William Clark to Secretary of War, May 18, 1807, William Clark Papers, MHS-JM.

21. *Ibid.*

22. William Clark to Secretary of War, October 24, 1807, *ibid.*

23. William Clark to Secretary of War, September 23, 1808, *ibid.*

24. Charles Jones, Jr., "George Champlin Sibley: The Prairie Puritan, 1782-1863" (Ph.D. dissertation, University of Missouri, 1969), 53.

25. William Clark to Secretary of War, September 23, 1808, in Carter (ed.), *Territorial Papers*, XIV, 226.

26. *Ibid.*

27. William Clark to Secretary of War, April 15, 1809, Letters Received by the Office of the Secretary of War Relating to Indian Affairs, Microfilm M-271, Record group 107, National Archives.

28. William Clark to Secretary of War, April 29, 1809, in Carter (ed.), *Territorial Papers*, XIV, 265.

CHAPTER V

1. William Clark to Secretary of War, October 24, 1807, William Clark Papers, MHS-JM.

2. William Edward Foley, "Territorial Politics in Frontier: 1804–1820" (Ph.D. dissertation, University of Missouri, 1967), 36–37.

3. *Ibid.*, 42, 50–52.

4. Hattie M. Anderson, "Missouri, 1804–1828: Peopling A Frontier State," *Missouri Historical Review*, Vol. XXXI (January, 1937), 157.

5. *Ibid.*, 156, citing Margaret Hunter Hall, *The Aristocratic Journey*, 278.

6. Anderson, "Missouri, 1804–1828," *Missouri Historical Review*, Vol. XXXI (January, 1937), 156–57.

7. *Missouri Gazette*, February 3, 1809.

8. *Ibid.*

9. Daniel DiPiazza, "A History of Federal Policy Toward the Public Mineral Lands, 1785–1866" (M.A. thesis, University of Missouri, 1957), 21–23.

10. Halvor Gordon Melom, "The Economic Development of St. Louis, 1803–1846" (Ph.D. dissertation, University of Missouri, 1947), 18, citing Thomas Ashe, *Travels in America*, 1806, 51.

11. Melom, "The Economic Development of St. Louis" (Ph.D. dissertation, University of Missouri, 1947), 27.

12. Lewis Atherton, *The Pioneer Merchant in Mid-America*, University of Missouri Studies, XIV, No. 2, 48.

13. Lewis Atherton, "Western Mercantile Participation in the Indian Trade," *Pacific Historical Review*, Vol. IX (September, 1940), 283.

14. *Ibid.*, 288–89.

15. John Mason to William Clark, December 31, 1808, in Carter (ed.), *Territorial Papers*, XIV, 247.

16. Sister Marietta Jennings, C.S.J., *A Pioneer Merchant of St. Louis, 1810–1820: The Business Career of Christian Wilt*, 65.

17. Frederick Bates to Secretary of War, September 28, 1809, in Thomas Maitland Marshall (ed.), *The Life and Papers of Frederick Bates*, II, 87.

18. Jennings, *Pioneer Merchant*, 55.

19. Richard Edward Oglesby, *Manuel Lisa and the Opening of the Missouri Fur Trade*, 17–32, *passim*.

20. *Ibid.*, 65, citing William Morrison Records, microfilm, reel 1, Illinois Historical Survey, University of Illinois, Urbana, Illinois, and Pierre Menard Journal, No. 15, 90, Illinois State Historical Society, Springfield, Illinois.

21. Oglesby, *Manuel Lisa*, 63.

22. Lewis' observations and reflections on upper Louisiana in Thwaites (ed.), *Original Journals*, VII, 369–88.

23. St. Louis Missouri Fur Company Ledger Book, 1809–1814, MHS-JM.

24. Oglesby, *Manuel Lisa*, 69–70.

25. William Clark to Secretary of War, August 18, 1808, in Carter (ed.), *Territorial Papers*, XIV, 209.

26. William Clark to Secretary of War, April 29, 1809, *ibid.*, XIV, 265.

27. John Mason to William Clark, August 11, 1809, Letters Sent by Superintendent of Indian Affairs, Microfilm M-16, Record group 75, National Archives.

28. St. Louis Missouri Fur Company Ledger Book, 1809–1814, MHS-JM.

29. *Ibid.*

30. *Ibid.*

31. Oglesby, *Manuel Lisa*, 75, citing Articles of Agreement between Meriwether Lewis, Governor, and St. Louis Missouri Fur Company, February 24, 1809, Chouteau Collection, MHS-JM.

32. Richard Dillon, *Meriwether Lewis: A Biography*, 321–27. Dillon speculated that the reason for Lewis' generous offer to the Missouri Fur Company for the return of Shahaka might have stemmed from the secret partnerships in the organization. Although Dillon's assessment may be accurate, his process at arriving at his conclusion fails to take note of certain possibilities. First, federal officials felt that seven thousand dollars was an enormous sum for the service to be performed. While this may also be true, it must be understood that frontier officials often overestimated the importance of their services—at least as compared to the federal government's view. In other words, it is very possible that Shahaka'a return, in Lewis' view, was of great importance because of the role that he could play as a friendly Mandan chief toward opening the Missouri River to the Americans, thereby bringing the Northwest into the American sphere. The importance of this national goal in the Northwest cannot be overestimated, and it may have stimulated both Lewis and Clark to co-operate with men such as Manuel Lisa, whose independent and narrow motives in trade had little nationalistic vision. Within this framework of understanding, the arrangements for the return of Shahaka seem less bizarre than is often thought.

33. Manuel Lisa to William Clark, July 20, 1809, St. Louis Missouri Fur Company Ledger Book, 1809–1814, MHS-JM.

34. *Missouri Gazette*, May 24, 31, June 7, 1809.

35. Oglesby, *Manuel Lisa*, 84, citing Pierre Chouteau to William Eustis, December 14, 1809, Pierre Chouteau Letterbook, 142, MHS-JM.

36. *Missouri Gazette*, May 10, 1810.

37. Oglesby, *Manuel Lisa*, 97, 98.

38. William Clark to Pierre Chouteau, February 20, 1810, Chouteau Collection, MHS-JM.

39. William Clark to Secretary of War, July 20, 1810, Clark Papers, MHS-JM.

40. MacFarlane, "Economic Theories Significant in the Rise of the United States Indian Factory System, 1795–1817" (M.A. thesis, University of Missouri, 1955), 123.

41. St. Louis Missouri Fur Company Ledger Book, 1809–1814, MHS-JM.

42. *Ibid.*

43. Oglesby, *Manuel Lisa*, 106.

44. Missouri Fur Company Articles of Association, January 23, 1812, William Clark Papers, XXX, Kansas State Historical Society, Topeka, Kansas. (Hereafter cited as KSHS.

45. Oglesby, *Manuel Lisa*, 123.

46. Missouri Fur Company Ledger Book, 1812–1814, William Clark Papers, XXX, KSHS.

47. *Ibid.* The Missouri Fur Company was again organized in 1819 with new personnel except for Manuel Lisa.

48. Oglesby, *Manuel Lisa*, 142.

49. Oglesby fails to recognize the importance of Clark's role in the company. The fact that Clark remained in St. Louis and did not actually travel into the field is no indication of his contribution. As already mentioned, Clark's knowledge of the region involved proved invaluable to the company, as did his knowledge of the current market information, which he could employ in selling the company's furs. In addition, the partners obviously recognized Clark's administrative talents and integrity by choosing him to remain in St. Louis to handle the company's affairs and later to act as president of the reorganized Missouri Fur Company.

In concluding that only Lisa had a "burning desire" to succeed, Oglesby gives insufficient weight to Clark's willingness to advance ten thousand dollars to make the company operative, the same sum that Lisa contributed.

CHAPTER VI

1. *Missouri Gazette*, May 28, 1814.
2. Tecumseh Oration, Draper Collection, Tecumseh Manuscripts, Typescripts, IV, 59, citing Arrell M. Gibson, *The Chickasaws*, 96.
3. Kate L. Gregg, "The War of 1812 on the Missouri Frontier," *Missouri Historical Review*, Part I, Vol. XXXIII (October, 1939), 16.
4. *Ibid.*, 17.
5. *Missouri Gazette*, July 25, August 8, 1812.
6. Julius W. Pratt, "Fur Trade Strategy and the American Left Flank in the War of 1812," *American Historical Review*, Vol. XL (January, 1935), 251.
7. *Ibid.*, 253.
8. *Ibid.*, 261.
9. Secretary of War to William Clark, April 18, 1813, in Carter (ed.), *Territorial Papers*, XIV, 655; Commission of William Clark as Governor, June 16, 1813, *ibid.*, XIV, 679. The Louisiana Territory had its name changed to the Missouri Territory along with a higher classification of second rank. This will be discussed in Chapter VI.
10. William Clark to Secretary of War, September 12, 1813, William Clark Papers, MHS-JM.
11. Gregg, "The War of 1812," *Missouri Historical Review*, Part II, Vol. XXXIII, (January, 1939), 199–200.
12. William Clark to Secretary of War, February 24, 1813, in Carter (ed.), *Territorial Papers*, XIV, 632–33.
13. Pratt, "Fur Trade Strategy," *American Historical Review*, Vol. XL (January, 1935), 262.
14. Gregg, "The War of 1812," *Missouri Historical Review*, Part III, Vol. XXXIII (April, 1939), 326–28.
15. Julia Hancock Clark to George Hancock, February 27, 1814, William Clark Papers, MHS-JM.
16. William Clark to Secretary of War, May 4, 1814, in Carter (ed.), *Territorial Papers*, XIV, 762.
17. Pratt, "Fur Trade Strategy," *American Historical Review*, Vol. XL (January, 1935), 264.
18. Gregg, "War of 1812," *Missouri Historical Review*, Part III, Vol. XXXIII (April, 1939), 330.
19. *Missouri Gazette*, May 28, 1814.
20. Gregg, "War of 1812," *Missouri Historical Review*, Part III, Vol. XXXIII (April, 1939), 334, citing Christian Wilt to Joseph Hertzog, August 6, 1814, Letter Books of Christian Wilt, Letter No. 125, MHS-JM.
21. William Clark to Secretary of War, December 11, 1814, William Clark Papers, MHS-JM.

22. Christian Wilt to William Hertzog Collins, October 11, 1812, War of 1812 Folio, MHS-JM.

23. Gregg, "War of 1812," *Missouri Historical Review*, Part III, Vol. XXXIII (April, 1939), 341.

24. *Ibid.*, 342.

25. *Ibid.*, 343, citing *Missouri Gazette*, May 27, 1815.

26. *Ibid.*, 344–45.

27. *Ibid.*, 346.

28. *Missouri Gazette*, July 15, 1815.

29. Gregg, "War of 1812," *Missouri Historical Review*, Part III, Vol. XXXIII (April, 1939), 347–48.

30. Joint letter, William Clark, Ninian Edwards, Auguste Chouteau to Secretary of War, September 18, 1815, *American State Papers: Indian Affairs*, II, 9.

31. William Clark to Secretary of War, October 1, 1815, *American State Papers: Indian Affairs*, I, 77–78.

32. *Ibid.*

33. *Ibid.*

34. *Ibid.*

35. William Clark to Secretary of War, November 20, 1831, William Clark Papers, IV, KSHS.

36. William Clark to Secretary of War, Otober 1, 1815, *American State Papers: Indian Affairs*, I, 77–78.

CHAPTER VII

1. *Missouri Gazette*, March 22, 1817.

2. In dealing with the whole question of intellectual change in the early nineteenth century, I found John William Ward, *Andrew Jackson: Symbol for an Age*, and James Willard Hurst, *Law and the Conditions of Freedom in the Nineteenth Century United States*, essential. In generally viewing intellectual change, I was methodologically influenced by Bernard Bailyn, "Political Experience and Enlightenment Ideas in Eighteenth Century America," *American Historical Review*, Vol. LXVII, No. 2 (January, 1962), 339–51, and also Gordon Wood, "Rhetoric and Reality in The American Revolution," *William and Mary Quarterly*, Vol. XXIII, No. 1 (January, 1966), 3–32.

3. Hattie M. Anderson, "Frontier Economic Problems in Missouri, 1815–1828," *Missouri Historical Review*, Part I, Vol. XXXIV (October, 1939), 40–41.

4. Foley, "Territorial Politics" (Ph.D. dissertation, University of Missouri, 1967), 185.

5. Anderson, "Frontier Economic Problems," *Missouri Historical Review*, Part I, Vol. XXXIV (October, 1939), 42.

6. William Nisbet Chambers, *Old Bullion Benton, Senator from the New West*, 70.

7. *Ibid.*, 71; Foley, "Territorial Politics," (Ph.D. dissertation, University of Missouri, 1967), 191–93. In addition to the treatment of Missouri territorial politics in the numerous texts on Missouri History, the most recent and comprehensive studies have been done by William E. Foley in "The American Territorial System: Missouri's Experience," *Missouri Historical Review*, Vol. LXV (July, 1971). Also see Foley, *A History of Missouri*.

8. *Missouri Gazette*, July 10, 1817.

9. William Clark to Thomas Jefferson, October 10, 1816, in Thwaites (ed.), *Original Journals*, VII, 398.

10. Anderson, "Frontier Economic Problems," *Missouri Historical Review*, Part I, Vol. XXXIV (October, 1939), 43.

11. Foley, "Territorial Politics" (Ph.D. dissertation, University of Missouri, 1967), 193–94.

12. *Ibid.*, 196.

13. More on the role of Missouri and William Clark in the War of 1812 can be found in: Gregg, "The War of 1812," *Missouri Historical Review*, Part I, Vol. XXXIII (October, 1938); and Pratt, "Fur Trade Strategy," *American Historical Review*, Vol. XL (January, 1935); and Edgar B. Wesley, *Guarding the Frontier: A Study of Frontier Defense from 1815 to 1825*.

14. Election certification by Governor Clark, September 19, 1816, in Carter (ed.), *Territorial Papers*, XV, 195.

15. *Missouri Gazette*, September 21, 28, October 5, 1816.

16. *Ibid.*, October 12, 1816.

17. *Ibid.*, March 22, 1817.

18. *Ibid.*, March 29, 1817.

19. John Ray Cable, *The Bank of the State of Missouri*, 50–58.

20. William Russell to Charles Lucas, February 22, 1817, Lucas Collection, MHS-JM.

21. *Laws of a Public and General Nature of the District of Louisiana, of the Territory of Louisiana, of the Territory of Missouri, Up to the Year 1824*, I, 397–400.

22. *Missouri Gazette*, March 29, 1817.

23. *Ibid.*, April 19, 1817.

24. *Ibid.*, April 26, 1817.

25. *Ibid.*, July 5, 1817.

26. *Ibid.*, July 26, 1817.

27. *Ibid.*

28. Frederick L. Billon, *Annals of St. Louis in its Territorial Days from 1804 to 1821*, 104–105.

29. *Missouri Gazette*, August 9, 1817.

30. *Ibid.*; John O'Fallon to Dennis Fitzhugh, August 11, 1817, William Clark Papers, MHS-JM.

31. *Missouri Gazette*, August 9, 1817.

32. *Ibid.*

33. *Ibid.*, September 6, 1817.

34. *Ibid.*, September 27, 1817.

35. Commission of Governor Clark, January 21, 1817, January 24, 1820, in Carter (ed.), *Territorial Papers*, XV, 233, 585–86.

36. *Missouri Gazette and Public Advertiser*, September 4, 1818.

37. Thomas Forsyth to William Clark, November 4, 1818, Thomas Forsyth Papers, MHS-JM.

38. *Missouri Gazette and Public Advertiser*, December 27, 1819.

39. Isidor Loeb, "Constitutions and Constitutional Conventions in Missouri," *Missouri Historical Review*, Vol. XVI (January, 1922), 190.

40. For a comprehensive treatment of change in order, law, and man's relation to governmental order, see James Willard Hurst, *Law and the Conditions of Freedom in the Nineteenth Century United States*. Of interest to the subject matter concerning value changes during the Jacksonian era, see John William Ward, *Andrew Jackson: Symbol for an Age*.

41. Rudolph Eugene Forderhase, "Jacksonianism in Missouri from Predilection to Party, 1820–1836" (Ph.D. dissertation, University of Missouri, 1968), 17–18.

42. *Missouri Gazette and Public Advertiser*, July 5, 1820.

43. Gordon Parks, "Factions and Issues in Missouri Politics 1820–1822" (M.A. thesis, University of Missouri, 1955), 56–58.

44. *Ibid.*, 15–16.

45. *Ibid.*, 56–58.

46. Marvin Cain, "Edward Bates: The Rise of a Western Politician, 1814–1842" (M.A. thesis, University of Missouri, 1957), 27.

47. Walter B. Stevens, "Alexander McNair," *Missouri Historical Review*, Vol. XVII (October, 1922), 10.

48. Elliott Coues (ed.), *History of the Expedition under the Command of Lewis and Clark*, I, lxiv.

49. *St. Louis Enquirer*, August 2, 1820.

50. *Ibid.*

51. *Ibid.*

52. Stevens, "Alexander McNair," *Missouri Historical Review*, Vol. XVII (October, 1922), 12–16.

53. *Missouri Intelligencer*, August 19, 1820.

54. *Ibid.*

55. *Ibid.*, August 26, 1820.

56. John L. Morrison, "A Historical Analysis of Fourth of July Orations, 1791–1861" (M.A. thesis, University of Missouri, 1949), 53.

57. *Missouri Gazette and Public Advertiser*, July 19, August 2, 1820.

58. *Ibid.*, August 16, 1820.

59. John O'Fallon to Dennis Fitzhugh, August 18, 1820, O'Fallon Papers, MHS-JM.

60. *St. Louis Enquirer*, August 30, 1820.

61. Thomas Hart Benton to John Scott, August 30, 1820, Benton Papers, MHS-JM.

62. Silas Bent to Secretary of State, August 29, 1820, in Carter (ed.), *Territorial Papers*, XV, 640.

CHAPTER VIII

1. William Clark to Secretary of War, March 1, 1826, *American State Papers: Indian Affairs*, II, 653–54.

2. *Ibid.*, II, 364–65; Secretary of War to William Clark, April 2, 1821, in Carter (ed.), *Territorial Papers*, XV, 712.

3. William Clark to Richard Graham, July 12, 1822, William Clark Papers, MHS-JM.

4. Angie Debo, *A History of the Indians of the United States*, 101–11, *passim*.

5. Francis Paul Prucha, "Andrew Jackson's Indian Policy: A Reassessment," *Journal of American History*, Vol. LVI (December, 1969), 538. Prucha, in his major work on Indian policy, *American Indian Policy in the Formative Years: The Indian Trade and Intercourse Acts 1790–1834*, generally carries on the same theme of continuity. No historian has more thoroughly analyzed American Indian policy from an administrative and political standpoint than Francis Paul Prucha; yet, even he failed to consider that the Enlightenment conception of the Indian deeply affected early policy and differed conceptually from policy prevalent after the War of 1812. For example, in an article defending Andrew Jackson's Indian policy, Prucha refers to early Indian officials, such as William Clark, as being equally as enthusiastic as Jackson about the distasteful policy of Indian removal. While Prucha correctly shows that Clark, like Jackson, did indeed enthusiastically support Indian removal, he fails to consider that Clark might have differed greatly from Jackson in his conception of what that policy would achieve and as to its effect on national development.

6. William Clark to Secretary of War, March 1, 1826, *American State Papers: Indian Affairs*, II, 653–54.

7. William Clark to Secretary of War, June 11, 1825, *ibid.*, 591–92.

8. James D. Richardson (ed.), *A Compilation of the Messages and Papers of the Presidents*, III, 1083.

9. *Ibid.*, 1252.

10. *Ibid.*, 1083.

11. Charles M. Wiltse, *John C. Calhoun: Nationalist, 1782–1829*, 170.

12. William Clark to Secretary of War, March 1, 1826, *American State Papers: Indian Affairs*, II, 653–54.

13. William Clark to Secretary of War, March 1, 1826, *ibid.*

14. George Dewey Harmon, *Sixty Years of Indian Affairs: Political, Economic, and Diplomatic, 1789–1850*, 157–66.

15. William Clark to Secretary of War, March 1, 1826, *American State Papers: Indian Affairs*, II, 653–54.

16. William Clark to Secretary of War, March 1, 1826, *ibid.*

17. Boorstin, *The Lost World of Thomas Jefferson*, 88, citing Barton, *New Views of the Origins of the Tribes and Nations of America*, vf.

18. William Clark to Secretary of War, March 1, 1826, *American State Papers: Indian Affairs*, II, 653–54.

19. William Clark to Thomas McKenney, December 10, 1827, William Clark Papers, MHS-JM.

20. Prucha, *American Indian Policy*, 252.

21. William Clark to Secretary of War, August 27, 1828, Letters Received by the Office of Indian Affairs, Microfilm M-234 Record group 75, National Archives.

22. Francis Paul Prucha, *Lewis Cass and the American Indian Policy*, 4.

23. Secretary of War to President of Senate, February 9, 1829, U.S. Congress, *Sen. Doc. No. 72*, 20 Cong., 2 sess., 1–2 (ser. 181).

24. Secretary of War to William Clark, March 10, 1829, Letters Sent by the Office of Indian Affairs, Microfilm M-21, Record group 75, National Archives.

25. William Clark to Secretary of War, November 20, 1831, William Clark Papers, IV, KSHS.

26. Prucha, *American Indian Policy*, 115, citing Upper Missouri Agency, Report of Andrew Hughes, October 31, 1831, *Sen. Doc. No. 90*, 22 Cong., 1 sess., 23–24 (ser. 213).

27. William Clark to Secretary of War, November 20, 1831, William Clark Papers, IV, KSHS. Francis Paul Prucha has challenged Clark's intentions in the above report by indicating that "These pious protestations of Clark to the Secretary of War in November 1831, however, lose some of their force when we consider that he was still granting permission to take large quantities of 'boatmen's' whiskey up the Missouri in the summer of the following year." (*American Indian Policy*, 117)

Prucha's evaluation of Clark's report lacks the perspective of an understanding of Clark the man and what he stated in the report. First, Prucha assumes that Clark's recommendations for total prohibition were law, then in fact they were suggestions for future incorporation into Indian policy. As the law stood in 1832, it was still legal to take liquor into the Indian country for use by the trading party. In his comments on Clark's continued allowance of large quantities of liquor in Indian country, Prucha implies that there was a consciousness or willingness on the part of Clark to allow such occurrences to take place. Such an interpretation, however, removes the series of events out of the context of their time. It does not, for example, consider the many devices which traders employed to deceive officials, such as the watering down of liquor once past a checkpoint or the brewing of liquor within the boundaries of Indian territory.

28. William Clark to Secretary of War, November 20, 1831, William Clark Papers, IV, KSHS.

29. Prucha, *American Indian Policy*, 250–73, *passim*.

30. William Clark to Thomas Jefferson, December 15, 1825, Vol. 230, Thomas Jefferson Papers, LC.

EPILOGUE

1. *Missouri Republican*, August 31, 1838.

2. Coues (ed.), *History of the Expedition under the Command of Lewis and Clark*, I, lxvii; John O'Fallon to Dennis Fitzhugh, November 2, 1821, O'Fallon Papers, MHS-JM; William Clark Diary, August 12, 1827, William Clark Papers, KSHS.

3. William Preston Clark to George Rogers Hancock Clark, February 27, 1833, William Clark Papers, MHS-JM.

4. Will of George Rogers Clark, November 5, 1815, *ibid.*; Will of William Clark, April 14, 1837, *ibid.*

5. *Missouri Republican*, May 3, 1827.

6. Lewis Collins, *Historical Sketches of Kentucky*, 446; Federal Writers Project of the Work Projects Administration, *Kentucky: A Guide to the Bluegrass State*, 221–29.

7. Will of William Clark, April 14, 1837, MHS-JM.

8. *Missouri Republican*, September 3, 1838.

9. *Missouri Saturday News*, September 8, 1838.

10. Kennerly, *Persimmon Hill*, 90.

11. *Missouri Saturday News*, September 8, 1838.

Bibliography

ARCHIVAL MATERIAL

Topeka, Kansas
  Kansas State Historical Society
    William Clark Papers
    St. Louis, Missouri Fur Company Ledger Book, 1812–14

Louisville, Kentucky
  Filson Club
    John O'Fallon Papers

Columbia, Missouri
  Western Historical Manuscripts Collection, University of Missouri
    William Clark Astronomy Notebook, 1805
    William Clark Memorandum Book, 1798

St. Louis, Missouri
  Missouri Historical Society-Jefferson Memorial
    Chouteau-Papin Collection
    Christian Wilt Papers
    George C. Sibley Papers
    Lucas Collection
    John O'Fallon Papers
    St. Louis, Missouri Fur Company Ledger Book, 1809–14
    Stephen Hempstead Papers
    Thomas Forsyth Papers
    Thomas Hart Benton Papers
    War of 1812 Folio
    William Clark Papers

Madison, Wisconsin
State Historical Society of Wisconsin
George Rogers Clark Papers, Draper Collection, Microfilm series J
Jonathan Clark Papers, Draper Collection, Microfilm series L
Thomas Forsyth Papers, Draper Collection, Microfilm series K
William Clark Papers, Draper Collection, Microfilm series M

Washington, D.C.
Library of Congress
Thomas Jefferson Papers
National Archives
Records of the Office of Indian Affairs
Letters Received, Record Group 75, Microfilm series M-234
Letters Sent, Record Group 75, Microfilm series M-21
Records of the Office of Indian Trade
Letters Received, Record Group, Microfilm series T-58
Letters Sent, Record Group 75, Microfilm series M-16
Records of the War Department
Letters Received by the Secretary of War, Record Group 107, Microfilm series M-271
Letters Sent by the Secretary of War, Record Group 107, Microfilm series M-15

GOVERNMENT PUBLICATIONS

American State Papers: Indian Affairs. 2 vols. Washington, D.C., Gales & Seaton, 1832–34.
American State Papers: Military Affairs. 7 vols. Washington, D.C., Gales & Seaton, 1860.
American State Papers: Public Lands. 8 vols. Washington, D.C., Gales & Seaton, 1836.
Carter, Clarence Edwin, ed. *The Territorial Papers of the United States.* Vols. XIV, XV. Washington, D.C., Government Printing Office, 1949, 1951.
Richardson, James D., ed. *A Compilation of the Messages and Papers of the Presidents, 1789–1897.* Washington, D.C., Government Printing Office, 1897.

U.S. Congress, Senate. *Sen. Doc. No. 72*, 20 Cong., 2 sess., 1–2 (serial 181).
———. *Senate Doc. No. 8*, 23 Cong., 1 sess., 77–79 (serial 245).

BOOKS

Atherton, Lewis. *The Pioneer Merchant in Mid-America.* Vol. XIV, No. 2 of *University of Missouri Studies.* Columbia, Missouri, University of Missouri Press, 1935.
Bakeless, John. *Background to Glory: The Life of George Rogers Clark.* Philadelphia, J. B. Lippincott Co., 1957.
———. *Lewis and Clark: Partners in Discovery.* New York, William Morrow & Co., 1947.
Billington, Ray Allen. *America's Frontier Heritage.* New York, Holt, Rinehart and Winston, 1966.
———. *Westward Expansion: A History of the American Frontier.* New York, Macmillan Co., 1949.
Billon, Frederick L. *Annals of St. Louis in its Territorial Days from 1804 to 1821.* St. Louis, Nixon-Jones Printing Co., 1888.
Bock, Kenneth. *The Acceptance of Histories: Toward a Perspective for Social Sciences.* Vol. 3, No. 1 of *University of California Publications in Sociology and Social Institutions.* Berkeley, California, University of California Press, 1956.
Bodley, Temple. *George Rogers Clark, His Life and Public Services.* Boston, Houghton-Mifflin Co., 1926.
Boorstin, Daniel J. *The Lost World of Thomas Jefferson.* New York, Henry Holt & Co., 1948.
Boyd, Thomas. *Mad Anthony Wayne.* New York, Charles Scribner's Sons, 1929.
Cable, John Ray. *The Bank of the State of Missouri.* New York, Longmans, Green & Co., 1923.
Cassirer, Ernst. *The Philosophy of the Enlightenment.* Trans. by Fritz C. A. Koella and James P. Pettegrove. Princeton, Princeton University Press, 1951.
Chambers, William Nisbet. *Old Bullion Benton, Senator from the New West.* Boston, Little, Brown and Co., 1956.
Chidsey, Donald Barr. *Lewis and Clark, The Great Adventure.* New York, Crown Publishers, 1970.
Cobban, Alfred. *In Search of Humanity: The Role of the En-*

lightenment in Modern History. London, George Braziller & Co., 1960.

Cohen, Yehudi A., ed. *Social Structure and Personality: A Casebook.* New York, Holt, Rinehart and Winston, 1961.

Coleman, Francis X. J. *The Aesthetic Thought of the French Enlightenment.* Pittsburgh, University of Pittsburgh Press, 1971.

Collins, Lewis. *Historical Sketches of Kentucky.* n.p., n.n., 1847.

Cooley, Charles Horton. *Human Nature and the Social Order.* New York, Charles Scribner's Sons, 1902.

Coues, Elliott, ed. *History of the Expedition under the Command of Lewis and Clark.* 3 vols. New York, Dover Publications, Inc., 1965 edition.

Cragg, Gerald R. *Reason and Authority in the Eighteenth Century.* Cambridge, Cambridge University Press, 1964.

Criswell, Elijah Harry. *Lewis and Clark: Linguistic Pioneers.* Vol. XV of *University of Missouri Studies.* Columbia, Missouri, University of Missouri Press, 1940.

Crocker, Lester G. *An Age of Crisis: Man and World in Eighteenth Century French Thought.* Baltimore, Johns Hopkins Press, 1959.

———. *Nature and Culture: Ethical Thought in the French Enlightenment.* Baltimore, Johns Hopkins Press, 1963.

Curti, Merle, ed. *Probing Our Past.* New York, Harper & Brothers, Pubs., 1955.

Cutright, Paul Russell. *A History of the Lewis and Clark Journals.* Norman, University of Oklahoma Press, 1976.

———. *Lewis and Clark: Pioneering Naturalists.* Urbana, Illinois, University of Illinois Press, 1969.

Dangerfield, George. *The Era of Good Feelings.* New York, Harcourt, Brace & Co., 1952.

Darby, John F. *Personal Recollections . . . During the First Half of the Present Century.* St. Louis, G. I. Jones & Company, 1880.

Davis, Richard Beale. *Intellectual Life in Jefferson's Virginia, 1790–1830.* Chapel Hill, University of North Carolina Press, 1964.

Debo, Angie. *A History of the Indians of the United States.* Norman, Oklahoma, University of Oklahoma Press, 1970.

Dillon, Richard. *Meriwether Lewis: A Biography.* New York, Coward-McCann, Inc., 1965.

Dorfman, Joseph. *The Economic Mind in American Civilization, 1606–1933.* 5 vols. New York, Viking Press, 1946–59.

Downes, Randolph C. *Council Fires on the Upper Ohio, A Narrative of Indian Affairs in the Upper Ohio Valley Until 1795.* Pittsburgh, University of Pittsburgh Press, 1940.

Eblen, Jack Ericson. *The First and Second United States Empires: Governors and Territorial Government, 1784–1912.* Pittsburgh, University of Pittsburgh Press, 1968.

Edwards, Richard, and M. Hopewell, M.D. *Great West and Her Commercial Metropolis Embracing a General View of the West and a Complete History of St. Louis from the Landing of Liqueste in 1764 to the Present Time.* St. Louis, Printed at the Office of the *Edward Monthly*, 1860.

Elkin, Frederick. *The Child and Society: The Process of Socialization.* New York, Random House Inc., 1960.

English, William Hayden. *Conquest of the Country Northwest of the River Ohio, 1778–1783, Life of Gen. George Rogers Clark.* Vol. I. Indianapolis, n.n., 1895.

Erikson, Erik. *Childhood and Society.* New York, Norton W. W. & Co., Inc., 1950.

Federal Writers Project of the Work Projects Administration. *Kentucky: A Guide to the Bluegrass State.* American Guide Series. New York, Harcourt, Brace & Co., 1939.

Flagg, John. *The Far West, 1836–37.* Vol. XXVI, Part I in Reuben Gold Thwaites, *Early Western Travels, 1748–1846.* 32 vols. Cleveland, Arthur H. Clark & Co., 1906.

Foley, William Edward. *A History of Missouri.* Sesquicentennial edition. Columbia, Missouri, University of Missouri Press, 1971.

Frankel, Charles. *The Faith of Reason.* New York, Kings Crown Press, 1948.

Gates, Paul W. *The Farmers Age: Agriculture, 1815–1860.* New York, Holt, Rinehart and Winston, 1960.

Gibson, Arrell M. *The Chickasaws.* Norman, Oklahoma, University of Oklahoma Press, 1971.

Goodman, Mary Ellen. *The Individual and Culture.* Homewood, Illinois, Dorsey Press, 1967.

Govan, Thomas Payne. *Nicholas Biddle: Nationalist and Public Banker, 1786–1844.* Chicago, University of Chicago Press, 1959.

Gras, N. S. B. *Business and Capitalism: An Introduction to Busi-*

ness History. New York, F. S. Crofts & Co., Inc., 1939.

Greenstein, Fred I. *Children and Politics*. New Haven, Connecticut, Yale University Press, 1965.

Hagan, William T. *American Indians*. Chicago, University of Chicago Press, 1961.

Harmon, George Dewey. *Sixty Years of Indian Affairs: Political, Economic and Diplomatic, 1789–1850*. Chapel Hill, University of North Carolina Press, 1941.

Heckscher, Eli F. *Mercantilism*. Trans. by M. Shapiro, edited by E. F. Söderlund. 2 vols. Rev. ed. New York, The Macmillan Company, 1955.

Heitman, Francis B. *Historical Register and Dictionary of the United States Army from its Organization, September 29, 1789 to March 2, 1903*. Vol. I. Washington, D.C., n.n., 1903.

———. *Historical Register of Officers of the Continental Army During the War of the Revolution, April 1775 to December 1783*. Washington, D.C., n.n., 1914.

Horsman, Reginald. *Expansion and the American Indian Policy, 1783–1812*. East Lansing, Michigan, Michigan State University Press, 1967.

———. *The Causes of the War of 1812*. New York, A. S. Barnes Co., 1962.

Hurst, James Willard. *Law and the Conditions of Freedom in the Nineteenth Century United States*. Madison, Wisconsin, University of Wisconsin Press, 1956.

Irving, Washington. *The Western Journals of Washington Irving*. Ed. by John Francis McDermott. Norman, University of Oklahoma Press, 1944.

James, James Alton. *The Life of George Rogers Clark*. Chicago: University of Chicago Press, 1928.

Jefferson, Thomas. *The Papers of Thomas Jefferson*. Ed. by Julian P. Boyd. 18 vols. Princeton, Princeton University Press, 1950–71.

———. *The Writings of Thomas Jefferson*. Ed. by Andrew A. Lipscomb. 20 vols. Washington, D.C., Published under the auspices of the Thomas Jefferson Memorial Association of the United States, 1905.

Jennings, Sister Marietta, C. S. J. *A Pioneer Merchant of St. Louis, 1810–1820: The Business Career of Christian Wilt*. New York, Columbia University Press, 1939.

Jensen, Merrill. *The New Nation: A History of the United States*

During the Confederation, 1781–1789. New York, Alfred A. Knopf, Inc., 1950.

Kennerly, William Clark as told to Elizabeth Russell. *Persimmon Hill: A Narrative of Old St. Louis and the Far West.* Norman, University of Oklahoma Press, 1948.

King, Edith W., and August Kerber. *The Sociology of Early Childhood Education.* New York, American Book Co., 1968.

Koch, Adrienne. *The Philosophy of Thomas Jefferson.* Chicago, Quadrangle Books, 1964.

———. ed. *The American Enlightenment: The Shaping of the American Experiment and a Free Society.* New York, G. Braziller Inc., 1965.

Lamar, Howard. *Dakota Territory, 1861–1889: A Study of Frontier Politics.* New Haven, Yale University Press, 1956.

Laws of a Public and General Nature of the District of Louisiana, of the Territory of Louisiana, of the Territory of Missouri, up to the Year 1824. 2 vols. Jefferson City, Missouri, W. Lusk and Son, 1842.

Lawson, Murray. *Fur, A Study in English Mercantilism, 1700–1775.* Vol. IX of *Toronto University Studies: History and Economics.* Toronto, University of Toronto Press, 1943.

Lewis, Meriwether, and William Clark. *Letters of the Lewis and Clark Expedition, With Related Documents, 1783–1854.* Ed. by Donald Jackson. Urbana, Illinois, University of Illinois Press, 1962.

———. *Original Journals of the Lewis and Clark Expedition, 1804–1806.* Ed. by Reuben Gold Thwaites. 7 vols. New York, Antiquarian Press Ltd., 1959 edition.

———. *The Journals of Lewis and Clark.* Ed. by Bernard De-Voto. 3 vols. Boston, Houghton-Mifflin Co., 1953.

Lovejoy, Arthur Oncken. *The Great Chain of Being.* Cambridge, Harvard University Press, 1961 edition.

Lowell, James Russell. *The Poetic Works of James Russell Lowell.* Boston, Houghton-Mifflin Co., 1890 edition.

Marshall, Thomas Maitland, ed. *The Life and Papers of Frederick Bates.* 2 vols. St. Louis, Missouri Historical Society, 1926.

Marx, Leo. *The Machine in the Garden: Technology and the Pastoral Ideal in America.* London, Oxford University Press, 1964.

Mead, G. H. *Mind, Self and Society, From the Standpoint of a Social Behaviorist.* Chicago, University of Chicago Press, 1934.

Merk, Frederick. *Manifest Destiny and Mission in American History: A Reinterpretation.* New York, Random House, Vintage Books, 1963.

Moore, Arthur K. *The Frontier Mind: A Cultural Analysis of the Kentucky Frontiersman.* Lexington, University of Kentucky Press, 1957.

Oglesby, Richard Edward. *Manuel Lise and the Opening of the Missouri Fur Trade.* Norman, University of Oklahoma Press, 1963.

Peake, Ora. *The American Factory System, 1796–1822.* Denver, Sage Books, 1954.

Pearce, Roy Harvey. *The Savages of America: A Study of the Indian and the Idea of Civilization.* Baltimore, The Johns Hopkins University Press, 1953. Later edition published as *Savagism and Civilization: A Study of the Indian and the American Mind.* Baltimore, The Johns Hopkins University Press, 1967.

Persons, Stow. *American Minds: A History of Ideas.* New York, Henry Holt and Co., 1958.

Philbrick, Francis S. *The Rise of the West, 1754–1830.* New York, Harper & Row Publishers, 1965.

Piaget, Jean. *The Language and Thought of the Child.* New York, Harcourt, Brace & Co., 1963.

Preston, John Hyde. *A Gentleman Rebel: Mad Anthony Wayne.* Garden City, New York, Garden City Pubs. Co., 1930.

Prucha, Francis Paul. *American Indian Policy in the Formative Years: The Indian Trade and Intercourse Acts, 1790–1834.* Cambridge, Harvard University Press, 1962.

———. *Lewis Cass and the American Indian Policy.* Detroit, Wayne State University Press, 1967.

Sampson, R. V. *Progress in the Age of Reason.* Cambridge, Harvard University Press, 1956.

Scharf, J. Thomas. *History of St. Louis City and County.* 2 vols. Philadelphia, Louis H. Everts and Co., 1883.

Schmeckebier, Laurance F. *The Office of Indian Affairs: Its History, Activities and Organization.* Baltimore, Johns Hopkins Press, 1927.

Schoolcraft, Henry R. *Travels in the Central Portions of the Mississippi Valley.* New York, J. & J. Harper, Printers, 1825.

Sheehan, Bernard. *Seeds of Extinction: Jefferson Philanthropy and the American Indian.* New York, W. W. Norton & Co., 1973.

Smith, George W. *History of Illinois and Her People.* 6 vols. Chicago, American Historical Society, Inc., 1927.

Smith, Henry Nash. *Virgin Land: The American West as Symbol and Myth.* New York, Random House, Vintage Books, 1959.

Sydnor, Charles S. *Gentlemen Freeholders.* Chapel Hill, University of North Carolina Press, 1952. Later edition published as *American Revolutionaries in the Making: Political Practices in Washington's Virginia.* New York, The Free Press, 1965.

Turner, Frederick Jackson. *Rise of the New West, 1819–1829.* New York, Harper & Brothers, Pubs., 1906.

Van Alstyne, Richard W. *The Rising American Empire.* New York, Oxford University Press, 1960.

Ward, John William. *Andrew Jackson: Symbol for an Age.* London, Oxford University Press, 1955.

Weinberg, Albert K. *Manifest Destiny: A Study in Nationalistic Expansionism in American History.* Baltimore, Johns Hopkins Press, 1935.

Wesley, Edgar B. *Guarding the Frontier: A Study of Frontier Defense from 1815 to 1825.* Minneapolis, University of Minnesota Press, 1935.

Wiltse, Charles M. *John C. Calhoun: Nationalist, 1782–1828.* New York, Bobbs-Merrill Co., 1944.

Woodard, C. Vann. *The Comparative Approach to American History.* New York, Basic Books Inc., 1968.

ARTICLES

Anderson, Hattie M. "Frontier Economic Problems in Missouri 1815–1828," *Missouri Historical Review*, Vol. XXXIV, Part I (October, 1939), 38–70; Vol. XXXIV, Part II (January, 1940), 182–203.

―――. "Missouri, A Land of Promise," *Missouri Historical Review*, Vol. XXX (January, 1936), 227–53.

―――. "Missouri, 1804–1828: Peopling a Frontier State," *Missouri Historical Review*, Vol. XXXI (January, 1937), 150–80.

―――. "The Evolution of a Frontier Society in Missouri 1815–1828," *Missouri Historical Review*, Part I, Vol. XXXII (April, 1938), 298–328; Part II, Vol. XXXII (July, 1938), 458–83; Part III, Vol. XXXIII (October, 1938), 23–44.

————. "The Jackson Men in Missouri in 1828," *Missouri Historical Review*, Vol. XXXIV (April, 1940), 304–34.

Anson, Bert. "Variations of the Indian Conflict: The Effects of the Emigrant Indian Removal Policy, 1830–1854," *Missouri Historical Review*, Vol. LVIV (October, 1964), 64–89.

Atherton, Lewis. "Western Mercantile Participation in the Indian Trade," *Pacific Historical Review*, Vol. IX (September, 1940), 281–95.

Bailyn, Bernard. "Political Experience and Enlightenment Ideas in Eighteenth Century America," *American Historical Review*, Vol. LXVII (January, 1962), 339–51.

Burk, Redmond, and Robert Kelley. "The Lewis-Clark Expedition Papers: The Genesis of a Case," *DePaul Law Review*, Vol. VII (1952), 162–171.

Clark, Harry Hayden. "The Influence of Science on American Ideas from 1775 to 1809." *Wisconsin Academy of Science Transactions*. XXXV (1943), 305–349.

Clark, William. "William Clark's Journal of General Wayne's Campaign," ed. by R. C. McCrane, *Mississippi Valley Historical Review*, Vol. I (December, 1914), 418–44.

Coman, Katherine. "Government Factories: An Attempt to Control Competition in the Fur Trade," *Bulletin of the American Economic Association*, Ser. 4, no. 2 (April, 1911), 368–88.

Curti, Merle. "Human Nature in American Thought: The Age of Reason and Morality, 1750–1860," *Political Science Quarterly*, Vol. LXVIII (September, 1963), 354–75.

DeVoto, Bernard. "An Inference Regarding the Expedition of Lewis and Clark," *American Philosophical Society Proceedings*, Vol. XCIC (August, 1955), 185–94.

"Donald Robertson's School, King and Queen County Virginia, 1758–1769." *Virginia Magazine of History*, Vol. XXXIII (April, 1925), 194–98; Vol. XXXIII (July, 1925), 288–92; Vol. XXXIV (April, 1926), 141–48; Vol. XXXIV (July, 1926), 232–36.

Dorsey, Dorothy B. "The Panic of 1819 in Missouri," *Missouri Historical Review*, Vol. XXIX (October, 1934), 79–91.

Easton, David, and Robert D. Hesse. "The Child's Political World," *Midwest Journal of Political Science*, Vol. VI (1962), 229–46.

Foley, William Edward. "The American Territorial System: Missouri's Experience," *Missouri Historical Review*, Vol. LXV (July, 1971), 403–406.

Gregg, Kate L. "The War of 1812 on the Missouri Frontier," *Missouri Historical Review*, Part I, Vol. XXXIII (October, 1938), 3–22; Part II, Vol. XXXIII (January, 1939), 184–202; Part III, Vol. XXXIII (April, 1938), 226–48.

Guiness, Ralph B. "The Purpose of the Lewis and Clark Expedition," *Mississippi Valley Historical Review*, Vol. XX (June, 1933), 90–100.

Horsman, Reginald. "American Indian Policy and the Origins of Manifest Destiny," *University of Birmingham Historical Journal*, Vol. XI (December, 1968), 128–40.

———. "Indian Policy in the Northwest," *William and Mary Quarterly*, Vol. XVIII (January, 1961), 35–53.

Jackson, Donald. "The Public Image of Lewis and Clark," *Pacific Northwest Quarterly*, Vol. LVII (January, 1966), 1–7.

Jones, Howard Mumford. "The Influence of European Ideas in Nineteenth-Century America," *American Literature*, Vol. VII (November, 1935), 241–73.

Kinkead, Ludie J. "How the Parents of George Rogers Clark Came to Kentucky in 1784–1785," *The Filson Club History Quarterly*, Vol. III (October, 1938), 1–4.

Kirkpatrick, R. L. "Professional, Religious and Social Aspects of St. Louis Life, 1804–1816," *Missouri Historical Review*, Vol. XLIV (July, 1950), 373–86.

Lindley, Harlow. "William Clark—The Indian Agent," *Mississippi Valley Historical Association Proceedings*, Vol. II (1908–09), 64–65.

Loeb, Isidor. "Constitutions and Constitutional Conventions in Missouri," *Missouri Historical Review*, Vol. XVI (January, 1922), 189–238.

McDermott, John Francis. "William Clark: Pioneer Museum Man," *Washington Academy of Sciences Journal*, Vol. XLIV (November, 1954), 370–73.

———. "William Clark's Museum Once More," Missouri Historical Society *Bulletin*, Vol. XVI, No. 2 (January, 1960).

McClure, C. H. "Constitution Making in Missouri," *Mississippi Valley Historical Association Proceedings*, Vol. X (July, 1920), 112–21.

"Missouriana: William Clark's Museum," *Missouri Historical Review*, Vol. XXVII (July, 1933), 344–47.

Pratt, Julius W. "Fur Trade Strategy and the American Left Flank in the War of 1812," *American Historical Review*, Vol.

XL (January, 1935), 246–73.

Prucha, Francis Paul. "Andrew Jackson's Indian Policy: A Reassessment," *The Journal of American History*, Vol. LVI (December, 1969), 527–39.

Rice, Howard C., Jr. "Jefferson's Gift of Fossils to the Museum of Natural History in Paris," *American Philosophical Society Proceedings*, Vol. XCV (December, 1951), 597–627.

Sheehan, Bernard. "Paradise and the Noble Savage in Jeffersonian Thought," *William and Mary Quarterly*, Vol. XXVI (July, 1969), 327–59.

Smith, Walter R. "General William Clark, Territorial Governor of Missouri," *Bulletin of Washington University Association*, Vol. IV (1906), 49–69.

Stephens, F. F. "Missouri and the Santa Fe Trade," *Missouri Historical Review*, Part II, Vol. XI (July, 1917), 289–312.

Stevens, Walter B. "Alexander McNair," *Missouri Historical Review*, Vol. XVII (October, 1922), 3–21.

Thruston, R. C. Ballard. "Some Recent Finds Regarding the Ancestry of General George Rogers Clark," *The Filson Club History Quarterly*, Vol. IX (January, 1935), 1–34.

Thwaites, Reuben Gold. "William Clark: Soldier, Explorer, Statesman," *Missouri Historical Society Collections*, Vol. II (October, 1906), 1–24.

Viles, Jonas. "Missouri in 1820," *Missouri Historical Review*, Vol. XV (October, 1920), 36–52.

Wesley, Edgar B. "The Government Factory System Among the Indians, 1795–1822," *Journal of Economics and Business History*, Vol. IV (May, 1932), 487–511.

Wood, Gordon. "Rhetoric and Reality in the American Revolution," *William and Mary Quarterly*, Vol. XXIII (January, 1966), 3–32.

NEWSPAPERS

Missouri Argus (St. Louis)
Missouri Gazette (St. Louis)
Missouri Gazette and Public Advertiser (St. Louis)
Missouri Intelligencer and Boon's Lick Advertiser (Franklin)
Missouri Republican (St. Louis)
Missouri Saturday News (St. Louis)

THESES AND DISSERTATIONS

Anderson, Hattie. "Thomas Hart Benton and Some Problems of the American Land System." Master's thesis, University of Missouri, 1920.

Cain, Marvin. "Edward Bates: The Rise of a Western Politician, 1814–1842." Master's thesis, University of Missouri, 1957.

DiPiazza, Daniel. "A History of Federal Policy Toward the Public Mineral Lands, 1785–1866." Master's thesis, University of Missouri, 1957.

Foley, William Edward. "Territorial Politics in Frontier Missouri: 1804–1820." Ph.D. dissertation, University of Missouri, 1967..

Forderhase, Rudolph Eugene. "Jacksonianism in Missouri from Predilection to Party, 1820–1836." Ph.D. dissertation, University of Missouri, 1968.

Jones, Charles, Jr. "George Champlin Sibley: The Prairie Puritan, 1782–1863." Ph.D. dissertation, University of Missouri, 1969.

Ksycki, Walter Joseph. "The Missouri Fur Company, 1807–1832." Master's thesis, University of Missouri, 1942.

Loos, John. "A Biography of William Clark, 1770–1813." Ph.D. dissertation, Washington University, 1953.

McFarlane, Larry A. "Economic Theories Significant in the Rise of the United States Indian Factory System, 1795–1817." Master's thesis, University of Missouri, 1955.

Melom, Halvor Gordon. "The Economic Development of St. Louis 1803–1846." Ph.D. dissertation, University of Missouri, 1947.

Morrison, John L. "A Historical Analysis of Fourth of July Orations, 1791–1861." Master's thesis, University of Missouri, 1949.

Parks, Gordon. "Factions and Issues in Missouri Politics 1820–1822." Master's thesis, University of Missouri, 1955.

Ronnenbaum, Sister Chelidonia. "Population and Settlement in Missouri, 1804–1820." Master's thesis, University of Missouri, 1936.

Index

Academy of Natural Science: 50
Albemarle County (Virginia): 13–14
American Fur Company: 74, 147
American Philosophical Association: 33
Armstrong, John: 33, 91
Arrow Rock (Missouri): 92
Austin, Moses: 70

Bank of Missouri: 114–16
Bank of St. Louis: 115
Bates, Frederick: 124
Battle of Fallen Timbers: 20, 24
Benton, Thomas Hart: 108, 116, 127
Biddle, Nicholas: 43
Big Bones Lick (Kentucky): 6
Billon, Frederick: 118
Blackfeet Indians: 80
Boonslick (Missouri): 89, 107
Brackenridge, Henry: 68
British: fur trade, 19, 25, 41, 72, 99, 102–103; Indian relations, 19, 65–66; exploration of the Northwest, 33–34; War of 1812, 87–103
Burr, Aaron: 53–54

Cabanné, Jean P.: 116
Calhoun, John C.: 137
Caroline County (Virginia): 12–13, 18
Carr, William C.: 116
Cass, Lewis: 144–45
Cassirer, Ernst: 5

Cedar Island (North Dakota): 80
Charbonneau, Toussaint: 42, 45
Charless, Joseph: 108
Chickasaw Indians: 153
Childhood Learning Theory: 159
Chinook Indians: 46
Chippewa Indians: 19
Chouteau, Auguste: 70, 75, 79, 97–99, 108, 110, 116
Chouteau, Pierre: 70, 75, 78–79, 83
Clamorgan, Jacques: 70
Clark, Ann Rogers: 13
Clark, Edmund: 12, 24, 28
Clark, George Rogers: 13, 14, 17, 25–30, 32, 44
Clark, George Rogers Hancock: 120, 151–52
Clark, Harriet Radford: 151
Clark, John: 17
Clark, John III: 13, 29
Clark, John Julius: 120, 151
Clark, Johnathan: 14, 17, 22, 29
Clark, Julia Hancock: 12, 94, 120–21, 124
Clark, Mary Margaret: 94, 151
Clark, Meriwether Lewis: 94
Clark, William: on Enlightenment influence, 3–6, 9, 12ff.; on museum, 6, 48–51; Indian Agent, 61–66, 75, 77, 95, 97; on Indian policy, 8, 56, 66, 129–39; Governor of Missouri Territory, 8, 9, 55, 68–69, 91, 99–100, 105–27; as Superintendent of Indian Affairs, 9, 129–50; his boyhood, 12–